Cambridge Elements

COMPLEXITY IN ECONOMICS

Simone Landini
IRES Piemonte, Torino
Giacomo Gallegati
Università degli Studi di Torino, Collegio Carlo Alberto, Torino, and Université Paris 1 Panthéon-Sorbonne, Paris
Mauro Gallegati
Università Politecnica delle Marche, Ancona

Shaftesbury Road, Cambridge CB2 8EA, United Kingdom

One Liberty Plaza, 20th Floor, New York, NY 10006, USA

477 Williamstown Road, Port Melbourne, VIC 3207, Australia

314–321, 3rd Floor, Plot 3, Splendor Forum, Jasola District Centre, New Delhi – 110025, India

103 Penang Road, #05–06/07, Visioncrest Commercial, Singapore 238467

Cambridge University Press is part of Cambridge University Press & Assessment, a department of the University of Cambridge.

We share the University's mission to contribute to society through the pursuit of education, learning and research at the highest international levels of excellence.

www.cambridge.org
Information on this title: www.cambridge.org/9781009547727

DOI: 10.1017/9781009547765

When citing this work, please include a reference to the DOI 10.1017/9781009547765

First published 2024

A catalogue record for this publication is available from the British Library.

ISBN 978-1-009-54772-7 Hardback
ISBN 978-1-009-54773-4 Paperback
ISSN 2732-5067 (online)
ISSN 2732–5059 (print)

Complexity in Economics

Elements in Complexity and Agent-Based Economics

DOI: 10.1017/9781009547765
First published online: December 2024

Simone Landini
IRES Piemonte, Torino

Giacomo Gallegati
Università degli Studi di Torino, Collegio Carlo Alberto, Torino, and Université Paris 1 Panthéon-Sorbonne, Paris

Mauro Gallegati
Università Politecnica delle Marche, Ancona

Author for correspondence: Simone Landini, landini@ires.piemonte.it

Abstract: Neoclassical economics is heavily based on a formalistic method, primarily centred on mathematical deduction. Consequently, mainstream economists became overly focused on describing the states of an economy rather than understanding the processes driving these states. However, many phenomena arise from the intricate interactions among diverse elements, eluding explanation solely through micro-level rules. Such systems, characterised by emergent properties arising from interactions, are defined as complex. This Element delves into the complexity approach, portraying the economy as an evolving system undergoing structural changes over time.

Keywords: complex systems, non-linearity, emergence, non-ergodicity, statistical equilibrium

JEL classifications: A11, A13, B1, B2, B4, B5, C6, C8

ISBNs: 9781009547727 (HB), 9781009547734 (PB), 9781009547765 (OC)
ISSNs: 2732-5067 (online), 2732-5059 (print)

Contents

Introduction

The 2007–2008 crisis was both a crisis of the real economy and a crisis of the dominant economic theory (Kirman, 2010). The question increasingly being asked is whether the 'Great Recession' is prodromal to the emergence of a new paradigm.

The road followed by economics is bumpy: the dominant economic model is fragile and weakly validated, and there is resistance to paradigm shifts. The alternative – very promising and adopted by many disciplines – is far from complete. There is a paradigm difference between standard economic theory and complexity theory. Standard economic theory is based on closed systems with agents that act independently, are homogeneous, and make rational choices, leading to economic results of static equilibrium or steady growth. Complexity theory analyses the economy as an open system, subject to new innovations and information, composed of heterogeneous agents with limited rationality giving rise to networks of interactions and institutions, and an outcome of disequilibrium characterised by continuous change due to innovation and imperfect and incomplete information. In such a case, the system is complex – that is, described by phenomenological laws that are not immediately descended from the laws describing the behaviour of the individual components.

The physics of complex systems has shown that equilibrium cannot be applied in the presence of irreversible phenomena, where the arrow of time matters (Waldrop, 1993; Nicolis and Nicolis, 2007). In the case of economic systems, the second law of thermodynamics is valid (Georgescu-Roegen, 1970) and, moreover, there are learning and interactions because there are informational constraints not contained in the price system. Reductionism and equilibrium are consequences of the closed-system functioning applied to the economy, considered as a structurally stable system, as often presented in standard textbooks: the economic process is reduced to a circular diagram with a peculiar movement between production and consumption (Georgescu-Roegen, 1970).

Innovation and informational limits stimulate agents to interact, and the way of interaction changes because of learning. Interaction takes place through changing networks of heterogeneous agents (Bookstaber and Kirman, 2018). Interaction produces emergent phenomena where the total outcome of a process is no longer the sum of the components (Anderson, 1972). If information is imperfect, because it is not homogenously distributed, there is room for interaction between agents with heterogeneous information sets. Accordingly, the mathematical framework to adequately model interaction is based on non-linearity, far beyond homogenous distributions and predictable proportional reactions to change.

The literature has claimed that the main elements causing structural dynamics are technological innovation (Griliches, 1979; Fraenken, 2006; Foster and Metcalfe, 2009; Antonelli, 2011; Bloch and Metcalfe, 2011) and knowledge (Fischer and Fröhlich, 2001). Complexity consists in the endogenous change of preferences and technologies made possible by the interaction of agents that act purposefully in a context shaped by non-ergodic processes (Antonelli and Ferraris, 2017). The key contribution of Schumpeter (1947), with the notion of 'creative destruction', as well as the contributions of the new growth theory (Romer, 1994), make an important step forward, although this assumes that the effect of knowledge spillover in terms of dynamic increasing returns is automatic. The contribution of Paul David (2000), regarding the distinction between ergodic and non-ergodic processes, points out that if the introduced innovation has success, it changes the ecology and the interactions, and creates new boundary conditions and a new information set. Consequently, it is no longer possible to use differential or difference equations in favour of the complexity and the computational approach (Thurner et al., 2018).

These arguments determine the existence of a structurally unstable system, analysed as a complex system (Arrow, 1994; Arthur et al., 1997; Arthur, 1999; Beinhocker, 2006). Complex systems are populated by many heterogeneous interacting agents. Moreover, structural instability entangles with path dependency, non-ergodicity, and learning. Time is historical, as it chronologically orders irreversible events, and the disequilibrium generated by that change – that is, the *primum movens* of capitalism – also drives the main analytical approach.

The non-equilibrium emphasises structural breaks: subsequent interruptions that come from agents that adapt to a situation that continuously changes. Complexity emphasises agents that react to changes made by other agents. Therefore, there can be aggregated equilibrium and individual disequilibrium. Taking this aspect into consideration certainly complicates the concept of equilibrium, because it introduces a variability that the general equilibrium model shuns and leads to the impossibility of rational expectations. Statistical physics has been used to overcome the limitations of a deterministic description in favour of a probabilistic one, whose states are not a priori but may change via interaction of heterogeneous objects.

The economy is a complex system, wherein the macroscopic outcome is not the mere sum of the micro-ones and the tools of the statistical physics become essential. The ordinary tools of the standard economist remain valid only for the very short period when the system can reasonably be assumed to be closed and its structure does not change. Moreover, human agents are, unlike atoms, thinking entities with free will. Agent modelling (Gallegati et al., 2024) thus seems the most suitable tool to analyse the behaviour of individuals, their interactions, and the emergence of empirical facts not found in individual properties.

Economics was born as political economy, to manage the change in society due to the advent of the industrial revolution. This happened before economics had the ambition to resemble physics and become a science (Mirowsky, 1989). One of the purposes of that classical political economy is to be useful to society to facilitate the process of growth and obviate the pathologies that it entails. If this purpose still has meaning, economics must equip itself with tools to look for the keys where they have been lost and not under a streetlight just because there is light there (Fitoussi, 2013).

As it has been understood in the hard sciences, complexity theory puts an end to the time of certainty, to the correspondence between cause and effect and predictability. As we will see, the dominant economic theory is based on the equilibrium and separability of systems, categories that are appropriated only for some systems of classical physics, which an economist would define as macroscopic. To study microscopic behaviour, statistical physics has introduced the probabilistic interpretation. There is then a contrast between a deterministic interpretation, which considers the equilibrium of each individual agent and therefore of the system, and a stochastic interpretation. According to this view, individual behaviour is random but leads to an equilibrium of statistical type, in which individual elements can be in disequilibrium while the system reaches a 'state of compatibility'. In the transition from micro- to macro-description, new facts emerge, which are not present at a lower hierarchy, for which the 'laws' are valid only at their specific level of disaggregation. For these reasons, the whole is different from the sum of its parts (Anderson, 1972), the properties of the whole derive from the interaction between the parts, and this implies non-linearity and uncertainty. This suggests the abandonment of the dream of being able to formulate a 'natural law', of the predictable proportionality between cause and effect and of the dynamics of a system that can be reconstructed as the sum of the effects of individual causes acting on individual components (Nicolis and Prigogine, 1977): it is a requiem for methodological individualism.

To link the micro-economy with the macro-economy, the *mainstream* approach introduced the framework of the 'representative agent' – an average isolated agent, who acts regardless of the behaviour of others – which is as analytically useful as it is fallacious and a harbinger of error. In this way, an attempt has been made to reduce the macro-aggregate to the micro-part by construction, which gives the idea of a possible, but false, micro-foundation – to say nothing of the impossibility of the analysis of income distribution, wealth, and agent size or, more generally, composition effects (Kirman, 1992). Nevertheless, though devoid of any ontology, the analogy is so convenient and effective that it is still used more than a century after its introduction.

The maximum–minimum (utility and cost) method derives from the analogy with classical systems of physics, deterministic and separable, and the principles that must be introduced are necessary (ad hoc) axioms to reduce the behaviour of economic agents to that of atoms. This happened around 1880 with the marginalist revolution of Jevons, Menger, and Walras, which aspired to transform the discipline of economics into a quantitative social science.

Almost at the same time, Boltzman's work was published and, shortly before, the second law of thermodynamics was formulated. On this basis, it was discovered that entropy always increases in closed systems, that matter and energy are neither created nor destroyed, but that every active process absorbs valuable resources (low entropy) and releases unhelpful waste (high entropy), and that this process is irreversible. The economic process cannot escape this physical law; in fact, even for economic processes the arrow of time matters – they are not circular but unidirectional – and irreversibly leads them from states of low entropy to successive states of higher entropy. Outside Newtonian determinism, where there is time symmetry, time matters. The neoclassical theory could not register the novelties of physics and limits itself to extending, axiomatically, the macro-perspective to the micro one, following a procedure disavowed by statistical physics.

The use of mathematics gave economics an authority that became a presumed objectivity and hid the identification of ideological reflections that precede the analytical phase in the social sciences (Schumpeter, 1954): the analytical construction of any economic theory is preceded by the ideological vision. This approach to economics is a decisive factor in the definitive affirmation of economic thought in the terms of the formal language of mathematics. For the first time, the axiomatic-deductive method is applied outside of the traditional contexts in which it had been developed (e.g., logic, arithmetic, geometry) and from which the natural sciences were able to take advantage successfully. Physics employs results that mathematics has axiomatically deduced in a rigorous way to formulate explanatory theories of the laws of nature and adopts them only after their empirical validation. A similar procedure is less common in economics, because of both the paucity of experimental data and the non-replicability of many events. For example, the real business cycle is the case of an economic theory incapable of explaining the facts but for more than a decade it was successful, even though the empirical evidence was in blatant contrast to the assumptions of the theory itself. There is no doubt that the behaviour of human beings is more difficult to describe through mathematical models than the behaviour of atoms. It is not sufficient to adopt the forms and methods of physics to model economics based on some analogy because agents are not atoms and economics is a social discipline that cannot disregard the importance of history.

Ultimately, there is an information problem: only in a closed, barter system – with complete markets and perfect information – do prices act as coordinators. However, when prices do not only reveal excess supply or demand, the market is no longer efficient (Grossman and Stiglitz, 1980). As we shall see, the general economic equilibrium model in the Arrow–Debreu formulation is not robust to minimal informational constraints. Both its 'optimal' theorems and economic policy suggestions are merely *logically consistent* mathematical exercises of an incorrect and *incomplete* system. Arrow and Debreu's model is mathematically unassailable if it is decoupled from the phenomenon to be described: an economy in search of equilibrium. The general equilibrium as an economic fact is transformed into a mathematical fact because of a set of axioms necessary to find the solution with a logically consistent procedure from the syntactic point of view, regardless of its correctness from the semantic point of view. This model is incorrect if we consider it as an economic model because it fails to describe any real economic system, although this was the original intention of the general economic equilibrium theorists. In formal terms, Arrow and Debreu's model is an admirable work that shows which and how many restrictions are necessary to find a solution to the problem of proving the existence of equilibrium. More than a descriptive model of the economy, it is an argument that shows the limits of thinking about economics through its abstract mathematisation, deprived of its phenomenology, without ontology but only by weak analogy. This is also true of the current dominant modelling: the dynamics stochastic general equilibrium (DSGE) models.

Economics is a social and evolutionary discipline. It deals with non-equilibrium complex systems, where the agents are numerous, heterogeneous, interacting, strategically thinking, and capable of learning. Their coordination comes from below, from the action of individual agents through the phenomenon of self-organisation. The dominant approach in economics adopts equilibrium as an ideal tool, implicitly assuming that economic systems are 'natural systems', whose empirical regularities do not change over time, so much so that we talk about 'natural laws'.

Table 1, from Axtell et al. (2016), highlights the main difference between the mainstream and the complexity approach to economics.

Non-equilibrium physics has shown that new tools are needed to analyse evolution. In this perspective, agent-ased modelling (ABM) is the methodology that seems most appropriate for studying a complex economic system (Gallegati et al., 2024). And so, just as equilibrium is a special case of non-equilibrium and linearity of non-linearity, we will see that the *mainstream* is a subset of complexity economics. This Element highlights that, since the economic system is complex, it can only be studied through a methodology appropriate to

Table 1 Contrasting perspectives on economic theory and models

Economic conception	Conventional representation	Complex, evolutionary approach
Number of agents	Representative (one, few)	Many (possibly full-scale)
Diversity of agents	Homogenous or few types	Heterogenous, possibly all unique
Agent goal, objectives	Scalar-valued utility, fixed	Other-regarding, evolving
Agent behavior	Rational, maximizing, brittle	Purpositive, adaptive, behavioral
Learning	Individual, social	Empirically grounded, group
Information	Centralized, free, uncertain	Distributed, costly, tacit
Beliefs	Coordinated for free	Uncoordinated, costly to coordinate
Interaction topology	Equal probability, well-mixed	Social networks
Markets	Walrasian, single price vector	Decentralized, local prices
Firms and institutions	Absent or unitary actors	Multi-agent groups
Selection operators	Single level	Multilevel
Governance	Median voter	Self-governance, rule evolution
Temporal structure	Static or equilibrium dynamics	Disequilibrium dynamics
Source of dynamism	Exogenus, outside economy	Endogenous to the economy
Properties of dynamics	Smooth, differentiable	Irregular, volatile
Character of dynamics	Markovian, path is forgotten	Path-dependent, history matters
Solution concepts	Equilibrium at the agent level	Macro steady-states (stationarity)
Multilevel character	Neglected, fallacy of division	Intrinsic, macro-level emerges
Methodology	Deductive, mathematical	Abductive, computational
Ontology	Representative agent	Ecology of interacting agents
Data	Simple, aggregate	Micro-data, Big Data
Policy stance	Designed from the top down	Evolved from the bottom up

From Axtell et al. (2016).

replicate (*in silico*) certain events that are unrepeatable in fact but can be simulated by constructing agent systems and studying their networks of connections (Gallegati et al., 2024).

In this Element, when we refer to 'economic theory' we refer to the dominant, or *mainstream*, economic theory. Moreover, by 'classical physics' we mean the physics that deals with non-relativistic and non-quantum phenomena. In the sections there are some boxes that deal with specific topics by fixing the main notions – those that can be recalled at various points in the text to facilitate the reading.

This Element is divided in two sections: *1 How Economics Came to Believe It Was a Natural Science; 2 Economic Complex Systems*. In Section 1 we deal with closed, non-complex systems characterised by equilibrium analysis. These are the economic general equilibrium systems inspired by classical physics from Walras to Arrow–Debreu to DSGEs (Section 1.1). In Section 1.2 we highlight the limitations of this general equilibrium model through some theorems formulated by the same economists who contributed to its formulation (Arrow, Debreu, Hahn), both by critics of its development as DSGE (Solow, Stiglitz) or by mathematics itself. In Section 1.3 we are interested in open systems and their inclusion in complexity economics. Economic system analysis can be split between closed and open systems, emphasising that only the former can properly use the tools of equilibrium while those of complexity must be applied to the others. Moreover, since economic agents are 'social atoms' (Buchanan, 2007) the theory becomes non-ergodic, from ergodic as it was in physics.

Section 2 is devoted to complexity. We first introduce some of the founding notions, such as statistical equilibrium and non-separable systems. Section 2.2 is based on self-organisation, scale invariance, and self-organised criticality. Section 2.3 aims at framing complexity economics, with attention to the notion of emergence.

This Element is accompanied by *Agent-Based Modelling: A Tool for Complexity* (Gallegati et al., 2024), also in this series.

1 How Economics Came to Believe It Was a Natural Science

Let economics not be afraid to become an axiomatic-deductive system,
assuming idealised economic agents and processes,
just as physics makes great use of entities such as rigid bodies,
inextensible and massless wires, perfect gases, frictionless surfaces,

Vilfredo Pareto (in Bischi, 2012, p. 10; our translation)

The year 1816 was a year without a summer because a meteorological anomaly, with the complicity of the eruption of the Tambora volcano in

Indonesia in the previous year, resulted in a sharp drop in temperatures (Schurer et al., 2019).[1] During that exceptionally rainy summer, Lord Byron's guests were forced to stay indoors for long periods of time, entertaining themselves with scientific-philosophical discussions and readings of stories about ghosts and other topics that always tickled the imagination. Among them was Mary Shelly, who wrote *Frankenstein*, a novel marked by many arts and philosophies of the past. Baron Victor von Frankenstein's scientific genius is caught up in the illusion that he can dominate creation, until he discovers that the 'monster' is, for him and the community, more a cause of repentance and terror than success. The same is true of *mainstream* economics. Theoretical conceptions and models have gotten as out of hand for economists as the creature got out of hand for the baron. In these models we find various characters, from various stories as realistic as they are unreal, 'as if' they had been written at Villa Diodati in 1816: the invisible hand, the occult auctioneer, the benevolent dictator, Laplace's demon, and the representative agent.

1.1 A Brief History of the Mainstream

It should first be noted that the 'pre-analytical' visions between *mainstream* and complexity economics are so distant as to be irreconcilable. The former deals with timeless closed systems, complete information, and non-interacting agents, modelled as if they were real barter economies. The latter deals with open systems and monetary economies, where information is limited and agents interact. The first aims to explain the exchange, the second is concerned with the genesis of profit.

The distinction between cooperative barter economics and monetary economics is due to Keynes, and he takes it from Marx. The barter economy is that of the allocation of given resources, of the exchange between, for example, a producer of apples who would also like to eat peaches and who, for this reason, seeks another who exchanges peaches for apples. If the producer wants milk, he must look for a milkman who wants apples. And so on for every good you wish to exchange. Money thus avoids recourse to barter. The same happens with banks that intermediate supply and demand for savings. Everything takes place in monetary terms for the same reasons mentioned here, and money is only a commodity that acts as a facilitator of trade.

In capitalism, what counts is credit (debt), not money, because it links today's investment to tomorrow's profit rate, thus opening the doors to dynamics. Similarly, banks are limited to intermediate between those who save and those who invest, transferring something already existing from one subject to another.

[1] 'Eighteen-sixteen was the year without a summer' (Rasputina; On Perilious World; Filthy Bonnet Co., 2007).

Production has already taken place and money – and banks – serve only to facilitate exchanges. Whether or not there are banks and currency, the result does not change: they are inessential to the general economic equilibrium models, both in Arrow–Debreu and in DSGE models. If barter is perfect, then there is no need for money. If there are frictions, then money is needed, but this assumes that there can be exchanges outside the equilibrium, which implies multiple equilibria all with different Pareto efficiencies, and which therefore come to be improvable – see the Greenwald and Stiglitz theorem (discussed later in the Element).

In a monetary economy, more money must be obtained from money, whereby the aim of production is not the satisfaction of consumers' needs but the realisation of a monetary profit. If one produces for profit, one no longer has the exchange of one commodity for another, but the transformation of money into commodity and again into money. Time enters the scene and money becomes capital. In the monetary cycle, money is used to obtain more money in the form of a monetary profit.

Banks produce credit. Compared to the barter-*mainstream* view, where banks are intermediaries of a commodity already produced between those who save and those who invest in a context that remains one of exchange, in a monetary economy money becomes endogenous – that is, loans create deposits (i.e., one lends what has not yet been produced).

The analytical inconsistency of the *mainstream* is illustrated by the so-called neoclassical aggregate production function, where output depends on the quantity of labour and capital, and how they combine (i.e., technology). But aggregate capital is not measurable, nor can the aggregate production function be obtained from that of the individual firms. Micro-foundation has a rationale only if agents are not identical in tastes, endowments, rationality, and information, when there is reason to have exchange and production of goods and services (i.e., not when the economy does not exist as its agents are all identical). *Mainstream* theories of capital cannot have an unambiguous theoretical measure of aggregate capital since it depends on the variable that capital is supposed to determine: the profit rate. It is impossible to give capital a measure in value that is independent of the profit rate. The reasoning would be circular because to measure capital we must estimate the profit rate, which cannot be estimated without knowing the value of capital.

The general equilibrium theory was formulated by Walras (1874), and later extended by Pareto (1896–1897 and 1906), inspired by the mechanical principles of Poinsot's *Elements de Statique* (1803). This theory aims to show that in equilibrium the system is efficient and optimal. Pareto-efficient allocation is the best possible situation in terms of allocative and productive efficiency: one cannot improve the utility of one individual without worsening that of another. Pareto efficiency does not imply a socially desirable distribution of resources and is independent of the equality or general welfare of a society. The Pareto criterion is not concerned with the fact that half of the world's wealth is in the hands of very few individuals.

One of the questions that economic theory tries to answer is how it is possible that, in a world of autonomous consumers and producers, there is coordination. How can it happen that inhabitants of a metropolis have the availability of drinks, food, and any other goods they need, every day, without a central coordinator? Walras's answer is simple. Coordination is made possible by the prices that are set in the various markets according to their relative abundance and that move upwards when demand exceeds supply, and vice versa. When the quantity demanded is equal to the quantity offered, prices do not change because equilibrium has been reached. And, among the many possible equilibria, there is one that guarantees the availability of a greater product at a lower price: perfect competition. Behaving selfishly, the individual agents coordinate in the aggregate. As Smith says – in very few passages in *The Wealth of Nations* (Roncaglia, 2005) – it is 'as if' there were an 'invisible hand' guiding them. Ever since mathematical formalisation entered economics, the system to be studied has been complicated but not complex.[2] The neo-liberal approach also upholds the principle of laissez-faire. The market works well on its own, and governments should only intervene when exogenous shocks significantly disturb its functioning.

For a demonstration of the existence of a set of prices that allows a Walrasian equilibrium, we must wait half a century until the work of Arrow and Debreu (1954). Debreu (1959) gives a (mathematically beautiful) axiomatic formalisation, while in Arrow and Hahn (1971) one finds the most complete exposition. Since then, the Arrow–Debreu model (Box 1) has become the reference for the *mainstream*, where each agent maximises its own objective function. The model aims to determine that set of prices where demand equals supply without any central figure coordinating production and exchange, but the equilibrium existence theorem gives no indication of how this is achieved.

The Arrow–Debreu model determines that set of prices such that demand equals supply without any entity coordinating production and exchange from above, thanks to the equilibrium existence theorem. The theorem merely establishes what are the conditions that realise it from a formal point of view. With little interest in realism, the economic problem has become a mathematical problem.[3]

[2] A complex system is an assembly of heterogeneous parts that interact within a relational structure that gives rise to phenomena that cannot be explained by the same categories that characterise their behaviour. The notion of a complex system will be taken up in Section 2.

[3] Hahn (1982) reiterates the impossibility of obtaining normative indications from the Arrow–Debreu model given the axiomatic basis on which it is constructed.

Box 1 The Arrow–Debreu (1954) Model

The Arrow–Debreu (1954) model collocates inside the Walrasian tradition to the general equilibrium and proposes a solution to Walras's original problem proving the existence of the equilibrium combining production, exchange, and consumption within a unified scheme by means of set-theoretical mathematical techniques. The model expands upon three primitive notions posited at the root of the economic system. Consider a finite number of commodities L; $\mathbb{R}^L$ is the commodities' space including labour. Consider a finite number of consumers M; $\mathbf{X}_m \subset \mathbb{R}^L$ is the set of available consumption sets of the m-th consumer: $\mathbf{x}_m \in \mathbf{X}_m$ is the generic consumption plan of the m-th consumer. Also, consider a finite number of producers N; $\mathbf{Y}_n \subset \mathbb{R}^L$ is the set of the available production or technology sets of the n-th producer: $\mathbf{y}_n \in \mathbf{Y}_n$ is the generic production set of the n-th producer. $\Omega \subset \mathbb{R}^L$ is the non-negative orthant of $\mathbb{R}^L$, hence $\Omega = \mathbb{R}^L_+$.

Production. Production is assumed to obey the following hypotheses. Every $\mathbf{Y}_n$ is a closed convex subset of $\mathbb{R}^L$ including 0: returns to scale are non-increasing and the possibility of no production is allowed. Defined $\mathbf{Y} = \sum_n \mathbf{Y}_n$ as the set of all the possible aggregate production plans, it is impossible to identify at least an aggregate production plan with at least a positive component if not even a component is negative – that is, without at least an input it is impossible to produce an output: $\mathbf{Y} \cap \Omega = 0$. Outputs of a producer are inputs of the production plan of another producer: $\mathbf{Y} \cap (-\mathbf{Y}) = 0$, therefore production is irreversible. Furthermore, from the production point of view it is assumed that each producer follows the profit maximisation principle, therefore it is assumed that a price system is given. Commodities' prices are normalised on the unit-simplex $\mathbf{P} = \left\{\mathbf{p} \in \mathbb{R}^L | \mathbf{p} > 0,\ \sum_h p_h = 1\right\}$: $\mathbf{p}^*$ is the equilibrium price.

Consumption. Consumption is assumed to obey the following hypotheses. Every $\mathbf{X}_m$ is a closed convex subset of $\mathbb{R}^L$. Preferences of the m-th consumer are defined by means of a utility function u_m that is continuous on $\mathbf{X}_m$ and so characterised: for all $\mathbf{x}_m$ it is possible finding a $\mathbf{x}'_m \neq \mathbf{x}_m$ such that $u_m(\mathbf{x}_m) > u_m(\mathbf{x}'_m)$ and if $u_m(\mathbf{x}_m) > u_m(\mathbf{x}'_m)$ and $t \in (0,1)$ then $u_m(t\mathbf{x}_m + (1-t)\mathbf{x}'_m) > u_m(\mathbf{x}')$. Moreover, every consumer is endowed with initial resources $\zeta_m \in \mathbb{R}^L$ and owns a share $\alpha_{m,n} \in (0,1)$: $\sum_m \alpha_{m,n} = 1$ of the profits of each producer. Therefore, for a given price system $\mathbf{p} \in \mathbf{P}$ the wealth of the m-th consumer is $\mathbf{w}_m = \mathbf{p}\ \zeta_m + \sum_n \alpha_{m,n} \mathbf{p}\ \mathbf{y}_n$.

Equilibrium. Depending on the previous assumptions, $(\mathbf{x}_1, \ldots, \mathbf{x}_M, \mathbf{y}_1, \ldots, \mathbf{y}_N, \mathbf{p}^*)$ is an equilibrium if it fulfils the following

Box 1 (Cont.)

properties: (i) $\mathbf{y}_n^*$ maximises $\mathbf{p}^*\mathbf{y}_n$ in every $\mathbf{Y}_n$ for all n; (ii) $\mathbf{x}_m^*$ maximises u_m on $\{\mathbf{x}_m \in \mathbf{X}_m | \mathbf{p}^*\mathbf{x}_m \leq \mathbf{p}^*\zeta_m + \sum_m a_{m,n}\mathbf{p}^*\mathbf{y}_n^*\}$ in every $\mathbf{X}_m$ for all m; (iii) given that $\mathbf{x} = \sum_m x_m$, $\mathbf{y} = \sum_n y_n$, $\zeta = \sum_m \zeta_m$ and $\mathbf{z} = \mathbf{x} - \mathbf{y} - \zeta$ it follows that $\mathbf{z}^* \leq 0$ and $\mathbf{p}^*\mathbf{z}^* = 0$.

Existence of equilibrium. The first Arrow–Debreu theorem states that for every economic system satisfying the preceding conditions it is possible determining a competitive equilibrium.

The second Arrow–Debreu theorem extends the first by means of the *abstract economy* notion, as a generalisation of the notion of game, with which the authors transform the competitive economy model into a game theory model. In such a way the theorem of existence of competitive equilibrium becomes a theorem of existence of a Nash equilibrium. In substance, the result is that 'an equilibrium point is characterised by the property that each individual is maximising the pay-off to him, given the actions of the other agents, over the set of actions permitted him in view of the other agents' actions' (Arrow and Debreu, 1954; p. 273).

In the Arrow–Debreu model there is no time, or rather it cannot be indexed because it is 'intrinsic'[4] (i.e., the same commodity produced or consumed at two different times defines two different commodities whose prices are determined). By stripping the notion of time of all chronological meaning, the dynamics are not foreseen and the arrow of time that explains the importance of history no longer makes sense. In Arrow and Debreu's model, equilibrium is a fact 'without history', determined instantaneously when the required mathematical conditions are met and which, from that moment, lasts forever. But the point is different: there can be only barter if information is perfect, evenly distributed among agents, and complete in time. Only under these conditions we can dispense with the existence of money, credit, time, and trust. The real discriminant argument with the non-*mainstream* approach is relative to information. If information is complete and the agents are rational, we can dispense with interaction, dynamics, and money. The whole economy is reduced to exchange, to barter.

The proof of the existence of equilibrium is a great achievement, but the problems of uniqueness and of unsolvable stability (SMD theorem; see Box 3) remain (Fisher, 2013). Without stability, one gives up all those exercises in

[4] This aspect is very clear in the formalistic approach of Debreu (1959), who accepts the idea of 'actual' infinity overcoming that of 'potential' infinity.

Box 2 Reductionism and Holism

According to reductionism the whole is the sum of its parts, while according to holism the whole is more than the sum of its parts. Reductionism is appropriate for the analysis of reducible systems while holism is appropriate for the analysis of irreducible systems. In extreme synthesis, as a first perspective we understand a system of parts, even interacting and heterogeneous parts, to be reducible if any part can be considered representative for inferring or studying the properties of the whole; when this is not possible, the system is non-reducible.

To exemplify a reducible system we can consider the solar system (macro): the planets are all different subsystems, of which we can identify different (micro) parts; they are mutually interacting due to the forces of gravitational attraction; and any planetary configuration is predictable only by basing itself on the laws that regulate their orbits around the Sun, either considering the barycentre of the planets or considering any other representative point: to describe the behaviour of the whole, the choice of its representative parts is irrelevant.

To exemplify a non-reducible system, we can consider a glass (macro) in which there are many water molecules, each composed of two hydrogen atoms and one oxygen atom (micro), in which there are also other particles in suspension, and all these heterogeneous parts interact by colliding randomly, even if the system is apparently at rest. In this case, it is not possible to choose a representative part of the whole to describe its behaviour because all of them together contribute to the dynamics of the system and none, individually, can explain its behaviour in a representative way.

One form of reductionism is theoretical reductionism: this is the case in which some special theories are absorbed by a general theory, the typical example being Kepler's and Galileo's laws that find synthesis in Newton's law. Epistemological reductionism considers cases of transformation of concepts proper to a certain discourse into concepts proper to a different kind of discourse: for instance, the mathematical formalisation of economic thinking transforms economic concepts into mathematical objects; this argument appears quite clear in the context of the Arrow–Debreu model (Box 1), but will become clearer in Sections 2.1 and 2.2, when we discuss the transition from reasoning about economics to reasoning about mathematics. An interesting example that shows the incompatibility of the two can be found in the reductionist attempt to base the whole of mathematics on axiomatic set theory, an attempt that Gödel's theorems (Box 8) have shown to be unfeasible by proving that in any recursively

Box 2 (Cont.)

enumerable axiomatic system true propositions can emerge that cannot be proved by remaining undecidable. From a holistic point of view, it is interesting to recall the thesis of the theoretical physicist Pierre Duhem, according to which the control of scientific hypotheses by means of verification or refutation cannot take place by means of separate experiments, but only within a global theoretical framework: 'The only experimental check on a physical theory which is not illogical consists in comparing the entire system of the physical theory with the whole group of experimental laws, and judging whether the latter is represented by the former in a satisfactory manner' (Duhem, 1954; p. 200). The logician Willard van Orman Quine argues that within the framework of a theory it is not possible to prove the validity of a single assertion without proving the validity of the theory. Consequently, since all scientific propositions are intimately interconnected, not even one theory can be proved without considering all the science that includes that theory. According to Quine 'our statements about the external world face the tribunal of sense experience not individually but only as a corporate body ... The unit of empirical significance is the whole of science' (Quine, 1951; pp. 38–39). These two perspectives find a synthesis in the Duhem–Quine thesis, according to which, not without controversy with respect to Popper's falsificationism (Box 12), no scientific hypothesis can be experimentally verified separately from a set of auxiliary hypotheses necessary to conduct the experiment, with the direct consequence that from any hypothesis one cannot make predictions without proving the correctness of the assumptions necessary for the test; for further discussion about Duhem and Quine's holism see, among others, Massey (2011).

comparative statics (i.e., the analysis of economic policy and fluctuations) for which economics was born. The abstraction required to prove the existence of equilibrium is formalistically correct, but pragmatically irrelevant, and therefore empirically useless. In fact, without time there is no way to account for innovations and no room for banks, money, and credit. In equilibrium, in the Arrow–Debreu model there is no room for money and the system is a barter model and everything is a commodity, even time and money, so much so that saving and capital accumulation are not contemplated. Everything is decided at the initial instant and there is no room for any of the factors that determine growth and evolution. On the other hand, if it is necessary to resort to the 'actual' infinite, then everything is fixed at the initial instant and nothing else can happen beyond what is prescribed from the beginning (i.e., from the beginning, the conditions for the existence of a perpetual equilibrium are set).

In the modern version of the general economic equilibrium (DSGE) time is 'extrinsic', explicit. It is no longer true that the same commodity at two different times defines two different commodities, and 'potential infinity' is considered, which makes it possible to reason about growth through dynamics. However, DSGE employs stochastic differential or difference equations to account for any perturbations around the expected trajectory due to exogenous shocks, but the initial conditions are influential, and time collapses at the initial instant. In the Arrow–Debreu model 'everything is given in a current way', always and forever. In the DGSEs, 'everything becomes in a potential way', but conditioned by the initial state defining, with it, some restrictions that must always apply while facing exogenous shocks. Thus, in the first case there is no dynamics, while the second case is determined from the beginning. It is like a rocket launched into space: from the moment of take-off, the trajectory is determined and, as time passes, it develops, but it is known. If disturbances occur, such as due to external factors or accidents of various kinds, the instruments on board and at the control base allow the trajectory to be adjusted to return to the predetermined trajectory given the initial and boundary conditions, to complete the mission. As we will see, such systems are characterised by ergodicity. Since they do not have an arrow of time, what happens in the short term does not affect the long term: there is only logical time and not historical, irreversible time (Georgescu-Roegen, 1971; Prigogine and Stengers, 1977). Under these conditions, the reference is that of classical mechanics, which works very well for some physical phenomena, but not for complex cases.

On the neoclassical front, the first contribution to the growth theory is that of Solow (1956). In his growth model, relations are established, from the beginning, between aggregate quantities, and it is shown that the system can reach a steady-state equilibrium where there is neither accumulation nor growth. What makes growth possible is technological progress, of unknown origin. To be able to speak of cycles and growth in a system of general economic equilibrium, we must wait for the theory of the 'real business cycle' (RBC; Kydland and Prescott, 1982) which attempts to micro-found the behaviour of aggregates. The integration of technological disturbances with growth introduces the possibility of fluctuating series. RBC theory considers the cycle as an equilibrium phenomenon, as the optimal reaction of economic agents. For this to be mathematically treatable, the system must be stable. This is a possibility that Debreu (1974) himself excludes by contributing to the formulation of the Sonnenschein–Mantel–Debreu 'theorem' (Box 3).

Box 3 The SMD Theorem

After the model of Arrow and Debreu (1954) (Box 1), generalised by Debreu (1959), the conditions for the existence of Walrasian equilibrium are known but two issues remain open: to demonstrate its uniqueness, and its stability. Based on the fundamental assumptions about the completeness of markets and the convexity of preferences and technologies, general economic equilibrium theory is well suited to the representation of economies populated by heterogeneous agents (Blume and Durlauf, 2000). Indeed, in the standard formal scheme, the description of the economy is micro-founded but the useful argument for application and comparison with the real world is the aggregate excess demand curve. Specifically to deal with the stability of the equilibrium, it is therefore considered necessary to find a link between the micro and the macro. Said otherwise, proven that for equilibrium to exist, the aggregate excess demand curve must be continuous, homogeneous of zero degree, and satisfying Walras' law, one wonders what properties of the aggregate demand curve are necessary, or even sufficient, to ensure the stability of general economic equilibrium and to what extent these properties are implied by individual preference patterns (Rizvi, 2006).

Using a simplified model, Sonnenschein (1972) concludes that any continuous real-valued function is an excess demand function, hence no restrictions on individual preferences are significant in determining aggregate excess demand. This initial limiting result for the development of the theory in the direction of uniqueness and stability is followed by two generalisations: those of Debreu (1974) and Mantel (1974).

The combination of these results leads to the so-called SMD theorem that Ackerman (2002) summarises as follows: 'almost any continuous pattern of price movements can occur in a general equilibrium model, so long as the number of consumers is at least as great as the number of commodities'. Given the general scope of this theorem, its consequence is that the theory is semantically incomplete (Blume and Durlauf, 2000), and syntactically incomplete (Landini et al. (2020)). Indeed, regardless of individual preferences or income distribution, the general equilibrium exists but is unstable and its dynamics can be as erratic, or even chaotic, as one wishes. Moreover, Saari (1992) explains that this instability is a property of the economy as a system, which emerges even if it is not found in any of its parts: thus, the system is not separable (Box 7) but is complex. If the introduction of even one new commodity is sufficient to generate instability, then not even Walrasian tâtonnement, as a price adjustment mechanism, is a guarantee of convergence towards the equilibrium which exists.

Box 3 (Cont.)

As Ingrao and Israel (1991; ch. XI) recall, Hildebrand gives a lapidary assessment that expresses the value of the scope of the SMD theorem: 'an economy of pure exchange can no longer serve as an appropriate prototype example of an economy if one wants to go beyond the problem of existence and optimality'. The SMD theorem is therefore a limiting theorem of the general economic equilibrium theory because it explains the impossibility of obtaining results in the search for the conditions of uniqueness and stability.

Shaikh (2016) shows that macro-outcomes are 'robustly insensitive' to the details of micro-processes – that is, insensitive to variations in the individual behaviours (Miller and Page, 2007; p. 46). This does not mean that micro-processes are unimportant; rather, macro-outcomes are different from micro-behaviours and aggregate properties can be generated by many different micro-behaviours. Therefore, a model replicating some macro-properties is not sufficient while the micro-foundation must be based on the micro-model ability to replicate micro-behaviours, not on their ability to replicate macro-properties.

On the intertemporal side with infinite horizon, the Boldrin and Montrucchio (1986) theorem (BM theorem), is similarly limiting for the development of the theory based on the representative agent, and therefore explicates its effects starting from the RBC theory to reach the modern DSGE interpretation. In the words of Stokey and Lucas (1989; p. 139) the BM theorem can be expressed as follows: 'Any sufficiently smoothed, first-order, autonomous difference equation can be thought of as describing optimal behavior through time.' Thus, 'a representative agent model can be constructed which replicates any set of aggregate time series on investment and consumption' (Blume and Durlauf, 2000; p. 20).

The stability of the equilibrium in the timeless Arrow–Debreu model is not proven, and further restrictions need to be considered it if we introduce time into the general equilibrium theory. Thus, if some shock can perturb 'today's' equilibrium, one cannot imagine returning to the same equilibrium 'tomorrow' because, in the meantime, the conditions of the system will have also changed. Because of the shock, a time-dependent system has new boundary conditions, which will characterise its evolution. On the other hand, if time is chronological (i.e., history matters), we cannot rely on a logical time that has the function of making the problem treatable with the mathematical methods of the theory of the complex systems.

By integrating Solow's model with Ramsey's (1928) optimal growth – extended by Cass (1965) and Koopmans (1965) – the necessary conditions for optimal savings are established in a model where households maximise utility and firms maximise profit. To do this, Ramsey assumes the presence of a 'benevolent dictator', which Barone (1908) had already shown to be equivalent to the Walrasian auctioneer. The benevolent dictator, by substituting himself for the market, succeeds in guiding the system along an optimal path.

Sixty years later, an attempt is made to replace Ramsey's original idea of the benevolent dictator with Muth's (1961) rational expectations hypothesis. Lucas updates Friedman's model (1969), which emphasises the monetary aspect of the neoclassical synthesis model by replacing the assumption of adaptive expectations with that of rational expectations and introducing Lucas' critique. Instead of a benevolent dictator who knows everything and pursues the economic well-being of his citizens, Lucas (1972) introduces 'rational expectations', according to which agents use information efficiently and without making systematic forecasting errors. The individual may make forecasting errors, but there is supposed to be a 'collective intelligence' capable of formulating correct expectations because it knows the true model of the economy and, therefore, on average, errors compensate until they cancel each other out.[5] Rational expectations are based on the assumption that individuals' subjective probability distributions are defined around an objective aggregate probability distribution.[6] This, rather than being an assumption, is an axiom because there is no probability theory that allows subjective probabilities to be transferred into objective probabilities, unless individual probabilities are linear and additive (Brady, 2018). Without bothering Bruno De Finetti (1931), who defines such an attempt as 'absolutely absurd' because objective probability does not exist, we are faced with the problem of the micro–macro relation, which is the stumbling block of all those theories that require aggregation. This will lead us to conclude that heterogeneity and interaction are at the root of the failure of Lucas' project of basing economic theory on individual behaviour to describe that of the aggregate. The consequence is that the approach of economic theory to equilibrium must be revised to adopt a complex one. This can consider that the interaction between agents produces emergence, irreversibility, and non-ergodicity that can be analysed only with heterogeneous interacting agent models (ABM; see Gallegati et al., 2024).

In the 1980s, the Lucas model was modified by what is called the real business cycle model, wherein agents have rational expectations, markets are perfectly competitive, but monetary shocks become real (technological),

[5] Assuming that, on average, errors cancel out implies the existence of an average, representative agent.

[6] Moreover, the system must be structurally stable (Lucas and Sargent, 1977).

allowing fluctuations around a growth path. However, their empirical validity has proven to be of embarrassing weakness. De Vroey (2015) reminds us that the RBC 'explanation' for the 1929 crisis is that workers were caught up in collective laziness. Attempts to 'resuscitate' RBC have failed. A now very popular development is the DSGE modelling approach, which introduces elements of imperfection into the system characterised by the optimising behaviour of consumers and firms with rational expectations. Compared to RBC models, DSGEs expand the range of stochastic shocks that can disturb the optimal dynamics of the economy. In Smets and Wouters (2003), Stiglitz (2018, p. 71) identifies a total of ten shocks: two 'supply' shocks, one productivity shock and one labour supply shock, three 'demand' shocks (a preference shock, a shock to the adjustment cost of investment and a government consumption shock), three 'push-cost' shocks (for the mark-up of goods, for the labour market and … for the required risk premium on capital) and two 'monetary policy' shocks and multiple frictions, including the 'formation of imitative consumption behaviour', a 'cost of adjusting the capital stock' and 'partial indexation of prices and wages that cannot be optimised again' so much so as to invoke the accusation of ad-shockery.

DSGE models are self-defined as Keynesian because of nominal rigidities – slow adjustment of prices and wages – embedded in a system derived from micro-foundations. They echo the spirit of what Joan Robinson called the 'bastard Keynesianism' of the IS–LM model, which introduces short-term nominal rigidities into an otherwise long-run neoclassical model.[7] Note that if prices do not move instantaneously the *mainstream* has two insurmountable problems because trade occurs in disequilibrium. First, it can no longer apply the rational expectations hypothesis that everything must happen in equilibrium. Then, if frictions are introduced there is a strong probability of transactions outside equilibrium. This means that the equilibrium reached will be path dependent: it will not be unique as it will depend on the dynamics outside equilibrium.

Rigidities in the short run, but not in the long run, lead to the false belief that Keynesian economics is valid in the short run and neoclassical economics is valid in the long run, and that a single model can describe both. But how can we have disequilibrium transactions in the short run that do not affect the long-run equilibrium in an ergodic system (Box 4) like the *mainstream*? In a letter to Edgeworth of 6 April 1891, Marshall argued that in the case of out-of-equilibrium trades, supply and demand can never reach equilibrium as a single point. The

[7] Versions of the DSGE before the 2007–2008 financial crisis exclude the banking and financial sector, on the assumption that finance and asset prices are simply a by-product of the real economy.

Box 4 Ergodicity

The term ergodic comes from two Greek terms: 'ergon' (energy) and 'hodòs' (route or path). The reference to energy, as we will see, finds historical-scientific motivations; today, we could refer to other properties of a system to consider their temporal evolution along some trajectory of the system (for a history of the concept of ergodicity, see Gallavotti, 2016). In mathematics, ergodic theory studies the ergodic behaviour of dynamical systems and consists of several theorems termed ergodic. Thus, when one says that a system is ergodic one should also specify with respect to which theorems the system is classifiable as ergodic.

The first results in the field of ergodic theory were developed within the framework of classical mechanics, deterministic and governed by ordinary differential equations, and can be traced back to Poincaré who, in 1890, when dealing with the equations of the dynamics of the three-body problem, formulated what is now known as the recurrence theorem, which explains how some dynamical systems, after a sufficiently long period of time, return nearby states already visited, sometimes even the initial one, an unpredictable number of times. Simplifying the matter, one could say that the systems that satisfy the recurrence theorem have no memory of their past because they retrace their steps without remembering that they have already been there: on the other hand, however, one cannot see why they should remember it and avoid passing through the same parts. Be that as it may, let's keep this aspect in mind, as it will come back later.

The general meaning of the ergodic theorems is that, under given conditions, a statistical property, described by a function, evaluated with respect to time (i.e., along the admissible trajectories of the system), is related to the same property measured with respect to the space of the admissible states: this space–time reference will also come back later. Physical systems that satisfy this general phenomenology are said to be ergodic: with some imprecision, those that satisfy it independently of the initial condition of motion are said to be memoryless. It seems, therefore, that Poincaré's recurrence theorem defines ergodic systems, but, with respect to the above phenomenology, there is a substantial difference: ergodic systems refer to statistical properties (i.e., the quantities to which they apply are described probabilistically), while the so-called 'recurrent' ones are deterministic. However, as we shall see, ergodicity is a notion very close to 'recurrence'.

The ergodic argument is developed in thermodynamics to relate the states of the individual molecules (the parts) of a gas to the temperature of the system (the whole) they comprise. Thus, this argument concerns the relations

Box 4 (Cont.)

between given quantities of the parts of a system and given quantities of the system. Since physicists realised that the microscopic description of a system like a gas, made of many interacting parts, is intractable with the methods of classical mechanics, they developed the method of statistical mechanics to face the new problems: this happened when, after having studied the macroscopic phenomena, physics became interested in the microscopic bodies that compose the matter of which the macroscopic ones are made. Thus, the systems of interest for the ergodic argument are mechanical systems characterised by statistical properties (i.e., evolving along statistically describable trajectories). Therefore, when we refer to the ergodicity of a system, we are implicitly referring to its behaviour in probabilistic terms, as is the case for a complex system.

The term 'ergodic' was introduced by Boltzmann in 1884 when he formulated the so-called ergodic hypothesis to explain that 'each surface of constant energy consists of a single trajectory. In other words, no matter what is the state of our system at a given time, it will pass (or has already passed) through any other state with the same value of total energy' (Kinchin, 1948; p. 52). Following this hypothesis, it can be deduced that the average behaviour of a system along a trajectory in time does not depend on the trajectory it is travelling along, therefore 'Using this conjecture it is possible to establish the coincidence between the time and phase averages on each surface of constant energy' (Khinchin, 1948; p. 53). In a slightly more general way, the average behaviour of a system can be considered with respect to any moment function of its probabilistic law.

Unfortunately, however, this hypothesis was falsified on logical grounds; in fact, contradictions were detected in its treatment, and it was passed to the so-called quasi-ergodic hypothesis, 'according to which every trajectory, although not filling completely the surface of constant energy on which it is situated, consists of an everywhere dense-point set (that is, it intersects every element of the surface)' (Khinchin, 1948; p. 53). Therefore, the mechanical-statistical reference of the ergodic argument is to be found in the quasi-ergodic hypothesis.

It was thus possible to better focus the argument by considering as ergodic that system which, on a sufficiently long time horizon, the time elapsed in some region of phase space, whose microstates – that is, a microscopic description of the positions and velocities of the constituents of a system on phase space (i.e., the microstate is the configuration at a given time of the parts with respect to their admissible states) – have the same energy or are

Box 4 (Cont.)

compatible with a given macrostate (i.e., a macroscopic description of the system through the probability distribution of its quantities with respect to a set of microstates) of the system, is proportional to the volume of that region so that each microstate can be visited by the system with the same probability. It is on the basis of this new description that one can consider that, for an ergodic system, the time average of a quantity coincides with the average of the same quantity evaluated on the space of the microstates. It is worth noting from the outset that a system that stays for some time in a region of its space of states has some degree of persistence: if this is infinite, the system has no memory of its past while currently living in its present.

In 'The ergodicity problem in economics', Peters (2019) synthesises the argument:

> We will call an observable ergodic if its time average equals its expectation value, that is, if it satisfies Birkhoff's equation
>
> $$\lim_{T\to\infty}\frac{1}{T}\int_0^T f(\omega(t))dt = \int_\Omega f(\omega)P(\omega)d\omega$$
>
> Here, f is a function of the system's state ω. On the left-hand side, the state in turn depends on time t. On the right-hand side, a timeless $P(\omega)$ assigns weights to ω. If [the] equation holds we can avoid integrating over time (up to the divergent averaging time, T, on the left), and instead integrate over the space of all states, Ω (on the right). In our case $P(\omega)$ is given as the distribution of a stochastic process. In systems with transient behaviour, that may require defining $P(\omega)$ as the $t\to\infty$ limit of a time dependent density function $P(\omega; t)$.

presence of 'rigidity' makes the system non-ergodic. In the non-linear dynamics typical of DSGEs, this is made inevitable by the fact that the dynamics depends on the initial conditions and, by definition, any shock changes the path by generating new initial conditions: a shock occurring 'today' changes the dynamics from 'tomorrow' onwards with respect to the one valid until 'yesterday'.

The rigidities mean that each long-run position is not independent of the short-run positions; the long-run depends on the path taken by the system during the transition from one position to another, albeit along a path of equilibrium, or at least presumed to be so because it is so constructed. Moreover, considering frictions requires abandoning the restful idea of the uniqueness of equilibrium and embracing that of multiplicity. The idea that the equilibrium position is not independent of the path followed by the economy is the subject of the most recent developments in complexity based on non-linear evolution and on notions such as hysteresis, path dependency, irreversibility, and lock-in effects, as we shall see in the next section.

1.2 Ergodicity and Criticalities of the *Mainstream*

According to Hall's (1976) apt definition, there are two types of economists: those of 'fresh water' (the Great Lakes, Chicago, Minnesota) and those of 'salt water' (Boston, New York, California). Different kinds because of the imperfections considered in their models, but still 'fish'. In fact, economists analysing the problem of information imperfections are a different animal, as the presence of incomplete and private information causes heterogeneity and interaction. These categories imply emergence, the marker of complexity, and are little cared for by economic theory.[8] But there is more: if there are rigidities in wages or prices, trade can also take place outside the equilibrium, and this implies that the system is non-ergodic as future trades should consider that the past ones happened out of the equilibrium path. Simplifying, we can say that there is ergodicity (Box 4) when two conditions occur: (a) the causal events in a series must not be excessively dependent on previous events, and (b) the probability distribution must be such that the averages over time and the averages over state space coincide.

In economics, the notion of ergodicity is important either theoretically or methodologically. In theoretical terms, the non-ergodicity of economic systems derives from 'radical uncertainty' (Keynes, 1921; Lavoie, 2004). In such a case, we do not have the essential information and knowledge about the system to be able to formulate expectations appropriately. This logic excludes the possibility of formulating probabilistically based expectations if the distributions of quantities are not known. In physics, by means of experiments, it is possible to deduce the distributions. In economics it is more difficult, and, for this reason, the a priori assumption of a probabilistic law is frequent, functionally able to specify a mathematical-statistical model that can be treated without a prior empirical check of the hypotheses. The problem is important because it has to do with the formulation of individual expectations. If over time the system evolves with its environment (i.e., changes its structure and with it the context), we cannot make predictions about the future. Assuming the invariance of the economic structure and the context to make deductions on the future is a risky operation because historical contexts are likely to be different and affect the economic structure at least as much as the latter affects the change in the

[8] Heterogeneous Agent New Keynesian (HANK) models for example talk to heterogeneous agents, even if there are two or more representative agents; see Kirman, (2019).

context. We could make predictions if the relations between the quantities at play in the system always remained those we have identified, regardless of the context, but history teaches us that this is not the case. For example, assuming that we know the preferences of a population of individuals in the early 1900s, we certainly cannot adopt the same information structure to predict what will happen in 2030 after two World Wars, a series of economic and financial crises, and the introduction of technological innovations that could not even be imagined in the Belle Époque, but which have historically and politically modified the behaviour of individuals and, therefore, of the system.[9]

Reality is generally non-ergodic. For physical systems all this fails because the laws of nature do not change, and time is only a parameter that indexes the succession of events. In economic systems individual processes change over time because time is irreversible and historical, and history is part of reality; indeed, it is that realisation that we cannot change, therefore it cannot be excluded from the model. The theoretical problem becomes methodological and, in practice, also raises a technical problem. A stochastic process is an infinite family of random variables indexed by a parameter with the meaning of time, while a time series is a finite sample of it. The process is non-ergodic if no time series exists that, regardless of its length, is sufficient to infer the probabilistic characteristics of the process. Under these conditions the process is said to have a very strong memory, meaning that the process is strongly persistent in each region of its state space. On the contrary, a process is ergodic if, as the width of the historical series increases, one can make better and better inferences about the probabilistic characteristics of the process and, therefore, one can identify an even larger set of its trajectories. The process has a weak memory, meaning that it has a weak character of persistence in some region of its state space.

In statistical time series analysis, a stochastic process is ergodic with respect to a parameter if the time sample estimate of the parameter converges to the parameter of interest with respect to some convergence criterion – typically, the quadratic mean. Any convergence criterion implies an asymptotic behaviour, made of successive approaches to conclude that, at infinity, the value of the parameter and its estimate will 'almost certainly' be identical. This implies the need to consider even longer time horizons of the sample to increase the

[9] In order to extrapolate a prediction, we should first 'know' (as if we were clairvoyant) the future by hypothesising the occurrence of the facts that contextualise the system (i.e., we should first formulate a context scenario to identify the space of the states to come, and then we should consider a family of probability distributions with which to assign to each state the probability that the system will pass through it). Put another way, we should follow a 'what if' logic by simulating future microstates to describe the context and then infer probability distributions of the macro-state. If this were possible, then the ergodic argument would make sense; otherwise, it would not.

information on the set of possible trajectories of the stochastic process. If the amount of information obtainable from the observation of the sample increases in time and reaches such a level as to be able to know a sufficiently large set of the possible trajectories of the process, then the process is ergodic. It does not persist in any zone of its space of states so that, in time, the sample observation becomes more and more useful to infer the properties of the process that generated it: future inference makes sense only for ergodic processes.

This result can be traced back to the ergodic argument developed in physics according to which, for an ergodic process, spatial and temporal averaging tend to coincide. That is, the longer we observe the system – ideally, to infinity – the larger the set of states that can be considered, so we can estimate a given parameter with respect to states at each instant and these estimates will converge to the estimate with respect to time along a trajectory. And this becomes an ergodic 'theorem': if knowing a sufficiently long time series is equivalent to knowing a sufficiently large number of time series, then the stochastic process is ergodic, and vice versa. For physical systems, whose laws of nature do not change, the abstraction of their asymptotic behaviour is a practicable method, but for economic systems, whose rules change over time because of innovations and regulatory interventions, then asymptotic behaviour is pure fantasy, as is any idea of ergodicity.[10]

We close this section by recalling some 'theorems' against the dominant economics formulated by *mainstream* economists or recognised by them as relevant and correct, although formulated by non-neoclassical economists, or mathematically untenable.

Let us start with the measurability of capital. The problem 'is to find a unit by which aggregate capital in value can be measured as a number; that is to say, a unit which is independent of relative prices and distribution and can therefore be included in a production function, where, together with labour, it can explain the level of aggregate production' (Harcourt, 1972; p. 23). Without the possibility of measuring capital, there can be no analytical measure of its distribution, nor of production or total factor productivity. In economics, a production function describes the combinations of factors (labour and capital) that technology allows to be chosen. Respecting many axioms (perfect competition and information, given technology, perfect substitutability between the factors of production), *mainstream* theory holds that for each level of production there is an optimal combination of factors such that factor prices are in a particular ratio: the 'substitution rate' of factors is equal to the reciprocal of the ratio of factor prices. However, if the factors' relative prices change then the proportions in which the

[10] Even if we assume that 'first principles' in economics are eternal, the interaction between economic agents brings about novelties that change the status quo, through the continuous emergence of techniques, markets, and products.

factors are combined also change. If wages increase and profits decrease, there will be a shift towards a factor combination that employs less labour and more capital. This proposition makes sense if there is only one capital good. With different capital goods we have the irresolvable problem of measuring them in value (i.e., pricing them). Sraffa and his school (Garegnani, 1970) have shown that in *mainstream* theory there is no univocal and negative relationship between wages and labour demand and between profit rate and capital, and that therefore there is always the possibility of a 'return of techniques'. It is possible that if wages rise,

> a given technique of production, which is labour-intensive, is replaced by another technique which is more capital-intensive; but at an even higher level of wages the first technique becomes profitable again and is thus in turn replaced by the one which had supplanted it … Thus it is shown that the prices themselves vary as the distribution of income varies, and thus the value of the capital that must be calculated from those prices varies. (Lunghini, 1991; our translation)

However, demonstrating analytically is not enough to convince those who have faith. Even though the most authoritative Cambridge (Massachusetts) neoclassicists have admitted that the aggregate neoclassical theory is logically contradictory, there are some who believe that it must be adhered to, and continue to be taught, for reasons of faith, while waiting for empirical verification that confines criticism to marginal and irrelevant cases. The lack of empirical relevance would not fix the analytical error. However, it is funny to note that when the lack of truthfulness of *mainstream* axioms (perfect competition, absence of information asymmetries and increasing returns) is pointed out by non-neoclassicals, the rejoinder is that the real economy behaves 'as if' it was the idealised one.

Moreover, there is no inverse relationship between wages and unemployment. Those who recommend that, in the presence of the unemployed, labour costs (i.e., wages) should be reduced argue this without an analytical basis to support it. If there are several types of capital goods, it is not possible to have a measure of aggregate capital, and hence neither an aggregate production function nor to derive it from the functions of individual firms because, generally, if the functions are non-linear the sum of the functions is not the function of the sums. The production function adopted by the *mainstream* is that of Charles Cobb and Paul Douglas (1928). It is a log-linear, homogeneous function of the first degree with two production factors: labour and capital. The equation tells us that output depends directly on how much labour and capital is used plus a 'residual' – that part of the output not explained by the increase in the production factors (i.e., technical change). Since an aggregate measure of capital is used, in the Cobb–Douglas production function the problem of measuring capital arises, aggravated by the fact that all capital available for production would be measured and not the capital used, which depends on market demand. Full utilisation of available capital can only be done at full employment. The Cobb–Douglas production function is also much criticised because its economic justification is based on unrealistic assumptions, such as perfect competition, absence of complementarity, and perfect factor divisibility – every time an entrepreneur succeeds in increasing production, unit costs fall, and returns are no longer constant. But there are other critical issues. The first is one of vision. The Cobb–Douglas function considers only two inputs (labour and capital) and neglects other inputs such as raw materials and reproducible or non-reproducible goods that are used in production. It effectively adheres to the myth of infinite growth in a finite world without regard to nature. The second is analytical. One of the major analytical weaknesses of the Cobb–Douglas function is the problem of aggregation. This problem arises when this function is applied to all firms in a sector and then aggregated to the whole economy. For a (production) function of several variables to be aggregable it must be additively separable into its components (capital and labour). This condition is not satisfied by Cobb–Douglas even when it is expressed in logarithms: $\log Y = \log A + a \cdot \log K + b \cdot \log L$. If the production function of each individual firm is Cobb–Douglas, the aggregate production function is not the sum of the individual functions; unless certain assumptions are made that contradict the underlying theory, the operation is mathematically impossible. The possibility of micro-founding is a myth that founds a wrong method. It should be recognised that the Cobb–Douglas function does not measure what it purports to measure since it is 'a law of algebra, not a law of production' (Dosi, 2023, p. 363).

In the light of the negative conclusions derived from the Cambridge capital controversies and the literature on aggregation, it is natural to ask why *mainstream* economists continue to use the aggregate production function and seek impossible micro-foundations: 'The younger generation of economists remains ignorant of these issues, with the consequence that bad habits and bad science breed bad economics and bad policy advice' (Felipe and Fisher, 2003, p. 211). Perhaps it is because the main role of *mainstream* economics and its method – DSGE – is to provide a fallacious apology for a social order that is presented as 'natural', but which in fact turns out to be unsustainable and unjust, creating social unrest and damage to the biosphere.

As mentioned, thanks to the fixed-point theorem (by Brouwer and later developed by Kakutani), Arrow and Debreu prove that the Walrasian model has an equilibrium. The result is highly relevant, but incomplete since the conditions of uniqueness and stability are missing. With 'heroic' assumptions uniqueness can be proved, and stability requires much more stringent assumptions. And if stability is excluded, neither fluctuations nor economic policy can be analysed, and the *mainstream* model loses all normative relevance.

There are two theorems – SMD and BM (Box 3) – about the impossibility of stability in the Arrow and Debreu model and in the optimal growth models respectively. The *mainstream* counter-objection is that 'stability is not a problem because the capitalist economy is stable'. It is reminiscent of the response of those astronomers who claimed that the planets were moving because they were driven by angels, and, indeed, the planets are moving, indifferent to our theories. The SMD theorem shows that the excess demand curve for a market with Walrasian agents can take the form of any function that meets the Arrow and Debreu criteria. Because of this approach, the market does not necessarily reach a unique and stable equilibrium point. Aggregate demand curves have an irregular shape, even though all individual agents are perfectly rational, because the quantity demanded of a commodity can increase when the price increases. Prices no longer coordinate. According to general equilibrium theory, the movement of prices (upwards/downwards when there is excess/shortage of demand) leads to equilibrium. If market demand curves have irregular shapes, even if all individual agents are perfectly rational, we can no longer apply the 'law' of supply and demand: we cannot assume that the demand curve for the market of a good, let alone the whole economy, is downward sloping because those of individual consumers are. The SMD theorem also raises serious doubts about the possibility of falsifying general equilibrium theory because models are the result of individual utility maximising behaviour where, as Mas-Colell et al. (1995) argue, 'anything is possible' – Gödel-undecidable, hence nothing can be certain and verifiable. As Werner Hildenbrand (1994, p. 169) reminds us, 'Until the SMD theorem, I had the naive illusion that the microfoundations of the general equilibrium model, which I had admired so much, made it possible to prove that this model and equilibrium were logically compatible. This illusion, but perhaps I should say this hope, has been shattered forever.' As the SMD theorem states, apart from unlikely conditions, the market demand curve can have any shape. To obtain a demand curve that shows that when the price decreases the quantity increases, it is necessary to purposely devise an implausible condition: income increases and one continues to buy the same things, just a little bit more. Of course, this is only plausible if there is only one person and one good on the market. Taking mathematics seriously, we can conclude that aggregate demand and supply curves cannot logically be derived from individual behaviour, since the interaction between individuals must be considered as an a priori determinant of the outcome. Only fideism's motivations can keep alive what, once and for all, logic says is dead. Morishima (1984) writes: 'If economists successfully devise a correct general equilibrium model, even if it can be proved to possess an equilibrium solution, should it lack the institutional backing to realise an equilibrium solution, then that equilibrium solution will amount to no more than a utopian state of affairs which bears no relation whatsoever to the real economy' (quoted in Kirman, 1992, p. 6).

A similar result to the SMD theorem in the timeless world of Arrow and Debreu is the Boldrin–Montrucchio (1986) theorem. It is applied to optimal growth paths – on which RBC and DSGE are based – which show that equilibrium prices and quantities can be chaotic, such that the optimal path cannot be determined and expectations may not be rational. Highly simplified intertemporal choice models can result in complex trajectories. Boldrin and Montrucchio show that economic agents who make decisions by solving optimisation problems over infinite time horizons do not behave in a smooth and predictable manner, since the time trend of optimal capital accumulation may exhibit chaotic tendencies. They show the way to all kinds of dynamics (periodic or chaotic), if consumers consider future consumption much less important than current consumption. An intertemporal model of optimal consumption with different capital goods thus generates chaos without violating the assumptions of traditional economic models. This means that the trajectories that rational agents must compute can have any degree of complexity that dynamical systems may exhibit. They can be chaotic, can have a sensitive dependence on initial conditions, and so on:

> If an economic model exhibits chaotic dynamics assuming that economic agents are rational, then of deterministic chaos they can in no way achieve in their predictions the infinite precision required to avoid the effects of the extreme sensitivity of chaotic dynamics. In other words, if we start with a model with rational expectations and find that it generates deterministic chaos, then the predictions cannot be rational of chaotic dynamics. (Bischi, 2012, p. 16; our translation)

A corollary that contradicts a hypothesis of the theorem![11] Again, the *mainstream* acknowledges that these problems undermine the analytical framework, but essentially removes them by arguing that non-uniqueness and chaos can be assumed to be quantitatively small – another 'theorem' that is 93 per cent true (Wilson and Pate, 1968). Even if macroeconomic quantities were not too chaotic, the problem of multiple equilibria – paths – cannot be easily solved since these appear in standard models with non-linearities. Besides Boldrin and Montrucchio, Benhabib and Day (1981) and Grandmont (1985) also show that chaotic behaviour can arise in many intertemporal models with maximising agents. This raises serious doubts about the methodological plausibility of the

[11] Our translation from a talk held by Bischi in 2018, titled "Modelli matematici in economia: una necessità, un periocolo o un'illusione?" www.mateinitaly.it/convegni/Venezia_2018/Materiale%20conferenze/Bischi.pdf.

concept of Walrasian equilibrium underlying these models. If the Walrasian equilibrium can only be established through the interaction of agents who must perform calculations that we know to be impossible, how can it be the foundation of a reliable model?

The theorem of Greenwald and Stiglitz (1986) states that the efficient market allocations envisaged by *homo œconomicus* theories cannot be achieved without government intervention if there are information imperfections and/or incomplete markets. The importance of the theorem is that in the *mainstream* literature it is assumed that markets are always efficient, apart from exceptions categorised as 'market failures'. The theorem shows that the exceptional cases are those in which the market is perfect. Markets are imperfect. The conclusion is that if markets are incomplete and/or information is imperfect there is no Pareto optimum and only government intervention can achieve it. Even ignoring the SMD and Boldrin–Montrucchio theorems, the axioms that the theorem reveals are too implausible for the *mainstream* to adopt. What's more, introducing imperfections into DSGE models makes no sense and comes at the price of giving up the uniqueness of the equilibrium.

The equilibrium paradigm, as applied to financial markets, is based on the axiom of efficient markets introduced by Louis Jean Baptiste Bachelier at the beginning of the last century and developed sixty-five years later by Eugene Francis Fama. This axiom states that the price of a security contains all available information. Paradoxically, however, either the information is perfect, and then there is no financial market, or, if the information is incomplete, no one would have any incentive to collect information and prices would not make the information public (Grossman and Stiglitz, 1980). Mandelbrot then pointed to the existence of power law distributions of prices, returns, and quantities of securities traded in financial markets. Such 'laws' – also valid in the real economy (Delli Gatti et al., 2007, 2008) – are generally characteristic of self-organised phase transitions or criticality (Box 10), both of which are correlated with cascading effects and fundamentally incompatible with the equilibrium concepts of the theory of efficient markets.

Let us close by reflecting on 'Hahn's problem' (1965). Arrow–Debreu's model cannot contemplate money and is a barter system, where money is a numeraire and banks – if there were any – are 'barter banks'. They intermediate between savers and investors in real goods: the farmer who has produced excess grain can lend it to another who uses it to sow it and the bank facilitates the matching. Since general equilibrium systems employ a general equilibrium concept based on the microeconomics of perfect barter, money and finance cannot be considered. Although these may be associated with the model, they are not essential; if removed, they do not change the equilibrium solution.

DSGEs are the most widely used models in academia and central bank research departments, even before the Great Recession, which, according to the vulgate, was due to the banks. The model is often blamed for not having predicted the crisis, but the problem is different. The real problem is that since there is no time, there can be no banks, no debt and no credit, so financial crises are not contemplated. Money and credit are 'additions' to 'real' Walrasian general equilibrium systems, as in RBC models. DSGEs are barter models masquerading as monetary models. When money is added to a model where it is not needed, logical errors and conceptual confusions occur. Money, which should facilitate trade, becomes a friction, a commodity produced by banks in a world where liquidity crises, bankruptcies, and domino effects do not exist. While before the global financial crisis the financial sector played no role in DSGE models, the Great Recession highlighted this limitation, and many aspects of the financial sector were incorporated into second-generation and subsequent DSGE models. Unfortunately, these incorporations are wrong because they do not address the fundamental flaw of these models.

Macroeconomic models such as Woodford (2003), on which the so-called DSGE-NK (New Keynesian) models are based, are barter models disguised as equilibrium monetary models built based on the real cycle and 'modified' with market imperfections. Many of the attempts made to improve the early DSGE models without the financial sector propose to eliminate barter features, which are held responsible for their failure to explain the Great Recession. What is specifically alleged is the treatment of banks as 'barter banks' – intermediaries that transfer real savings from savers to investors. When Jakab and Kumhof (2015) propose to replace the 'barter banks' in the DSGE model with banks that create deposits out of thin air they leave the model's perfect microeconomic foundations intact. The financial system and banks are modelled as optimisation problems subject to layers of constraints, such as adjustment costs, and a host of other imperfections and frictions relevant in a monetary economy. But banks are not required to make 'loans' in the model because such a role is not required under the microeconomic foundations of Arrow and Debreu given that everything happens in the initial instant. Benes et al. (2014) and Jakab and Kumhof (2015) propose to circumvent the barter properties of the DSGE model by incorporating the feature of contemporary monetary systems that loans create deposits and thus create money. But this amendment does not solve the problem posed by Hahn; it simply replaces a non-essential addition to the model with another (albeit more correct) one. It therefore leaves in place the logical fallacy and conceptual confusions that arise from misusing the microeconomic underpinnings of the old DSGE model. The new 'financial constraint' is a non-essential or redundant addition to the model, so that the growth path does not change and is neither consistent nor complete from the point of view of stock-flow consistency. All the relevant realism introduced in financial sector analysis falls away if the financial constraint is redundant. The 'financial constraint' can be removed, leaving a perfect barter equilibrium typical of general equilibrium analysis. The same applies to other frictions incorporated in DSGE models. In a nutshell, the models of the saltwater economists – DSGE-NK – are based on those of the freshwater economists – RBC – and share with them the vision of a barter economy.

1.3 It Takes a Change of Paradigm

Economics has taken physics – classical mechanics – as its model, where the laws of phenomena and bodies' interactions never change. However, we know that one of the characteristics of the stylised emerging facts of economics is precisely that they change over time. When it comes to methodological implementation, the *mainstream* argues that there is a close analogy between economics and the physics of mechanical systems. As Georgescu-Roegen (1971) thought, this is an almost curious event. When the mechanistic dogma was losing its supremacy in physics and philosophy, the founders of neoclassical thought in economics assumed it as foundational and, since then, little has changed. The link between the two disciplines can be identified in the principle of minimising effort to obtain the maximum result, which permeates classical physics based on infinitesimal calculus. Pareto (1896–1897) set out to 'de-pollute' the social sciences from politics and philosophy, taking analytical mechanics as its model: 'Let economics not be afraid to become an axiomatic-deductive system, assuming idealised economic agents and processes, just as physics makes great use of entities such as rigid bodies, inextensible and massless wires, perfect gases, frictionless surfaces' (Bischi, 2012, p. 10; our translation). However, while in physics the 'idealisations' of which Pareto speaks are simplifications of 'reality as it is' to arrive at models capable of replicating reality itself with a good margin of approximation, some economic hypotheses (e.g., equilibrium, complete markets, perfect information, representative agent) are not simplifications but ideological constructions.

This leads to the question of whether it is possible to transform a human science – a discipline whose procedures and conclusions heavily involve historical, cultural, and political prejudices – into a quantitative one. Moreover, calculation may not exhaust the determination of the whole of economic phenomena. If so, there would be the non-mathematical problem of finding the limit of the use of mathematical methods. The use of mathematics provides economics with a particular authority but, as Debreu warns, 'the seduction of mathematical form can become almost irresistible. In the pursuit of such a form, the researcher may be tempted to forget the economic content and to avoid such economic content and to avoid those economic problems which are not directly subject to mathematisation' (Bischi (2012), p. 10; our translation). The increasingly abstract formalisation of these models, often due to the need for simplification to make them 'analytically tractable', to the point of committing what Akerlof (2020) calls 'sins of omission', together with their difficulty in explaining certain observed economic and social phenomena, has led to questions about the usefulness of tools that sometimes seem to be used as an end in themselves. Mathematical methods and reasonings of physics are not enough to understand and explain economics' facts and phenomena such as agents' motivations, expectations, and psychology: economics is a moral science. In a 1938 letter 'on Tinbergen to Harrod' Keynes writes that

> [The point needs emphasising because] the art of thinking in terms of models is a difficult – largely because it is an unaccustomed – practice. The pseudo-analogy with the physical sciences leads directly counter to the habit of mind which is most important for an economist proper to acquire. I also want to emphasise strongly the point about economics being a moral science. I mentioned before that it deals with introspection and with values. I might have added that it deals with motives, expectations, psychological uncertainties. One has to be constantly on guard against treating the material as constant and homogeneous. It is as though the fall of the apple to the ground depended on the apple's motives, on whether it is worth while falling to the ground, and whether the ground wanted the apple to fall, and on mistaken calculations on the part of the apple as to how far it was from the centre of the earth. (Keynes, 1973; vol. XIV, p. 300)

Something similar is proposed by Feynmann (2002) when he argues that social sciences are not sciences, but disciplines that adopt the forms of science without doing science because they cannot discover laws in fact, it is not likely to discover laws in systems where they cannot exist.

In *History of Economic Analysis*, Schumpeter emphasises that in perfect competition, when agents are individually irrelevant to the system, the principle of 'strategy exclusion' applies. Whenever we abandon the axiom of perfect competition to introduce sticky price or wage adjustments, we introduce the need to model interaction. The only way to do this is by means of a network in which the nodes are the agents, and the links are the relationships between them. One interacts with others only if there is heterogeneity in tastes and endowments, whereas there is strategic interaction – the game theory of von Neumann and Morgenstern (1947) and Nash (1950) – with information differentials. The economic literature distinguishes between the two cases by speaking of weak (without interaction) and strong (with interaction) heterogeneity. The difference means that the two approaches are not comparable because interaction gives rise to phenomena (domino effects, imitation, scale-free events, fat-tailed distributions, etc.) that any model with heterogeneous agents (e.g., the HANK model merely incorporates heterogeneity and uninsurable idiosyncratic risk into the models) cannot capture by construction. In the presence of strategic interaction, the equilibrium that is obtained is not the Walrasian equilibrium, efficient and optimal, but rather the Nash equilibrium that depends on the strategies adopted.

While complex systems are non-separable, in order for the various components to interact, classical systems are separable and the properties can be added (Box 7). The aggregate result is no more than the sum of the effects considered separately, and no characteristics emerge that are not already present in the individual elements. If the elements depend on each other, then the whole is different from the sum of the parts and characteristics appear that do not belong to any of the individual constituents (Anderson, 1972). The non-linearity relevant to complexity is not that of the single function, but that producing emergence and that follows from interaction. It is not a mere mathematical-formal point, relating to the functions that are adopted, but rather to the forms and modes of the structural evolution of the system and how the network of relations between agents is made and changes.

Emergent behaviour (Box 11) is characteristic of complex systems, made of particles or living organisms, social or economic individuals. Emergence belies the reductionist view that all scientific knowledge can be traced back to the laws of the elementary parts of the whole. Complexity has shown that, as one moves up the dimensional scale (particles, atoms, molecules, organisms, etc.), new laws emerge that do not exist in the lower levels of the structural hierarchy. Complexity now embraces many disciplines and is being successfully applied in management and finance, but in economics it is meeting with much resistance. On the other hand, the perspective of complexity unhinges some of the certainties of dominant economic thinking and lends itself very well to revealing its fragility and inconsistency.

In the presence of information asymmetries, agents interact by forming new markets and institutions. Social systems change and evolve over time because there are interactions and innovations, while individual agents act through the process of self-organisation. Individuals solve problems by coordinating, often creating new institutions that solve some problems and change the system. Thus, the economy with a central bank or with futures markets or with an interbank market is different from the economy without them and produces different outcomes. Only the complexity that sees the economy as a continuously evolving system can provide adequate answers. At this point the meaning of what Marshall wrote in the *Principles* should be clear: 'the Mecca of the economist lies in economic biology rather than in economic dynamics'.[12] The economy is an evolutionary process dominated by technological innovation, markets' rules, and individuals' behaviour and preferences. All these processes are intrinsic in all economic and human systems that are irreversible, such that there can be no analogue with the mechanistic paradigm where the laws never change (Brinley, 1991; Hodgson, 1993). Since information can only be limited and incomplete, strategic interaction is produced, so that biology itself is superseded by a discipline with thinking agents.

Much of current economic theory is designed according to the principle that, being a science of nature like physics, it has immutable laws and agents are seen as independent 'atoms'. Unlike economic agents, atoms have no information problems and therefore do not think or learn. The assumptions of perfect information and complete rationality may be of some use at the beginning of theoretical speculation, but is of no normative relevance.

Assuming these hypotheses to be valid – that is, axiomatically – one ends up eliminating, by construction, all pathologies. Reviewing Edgeworth's (1881) *Mathematical Psychics: An Essay on the Application of Mathematics to the Moral Sciences*, Marshall (1881) writes that it will be interesting to see whether in the future the author will be able to control the equations or run away with them. With different words, Sraffa (1932a, b) intervenes in the debate between Keynes and Hayek and recalls how the conclusions reached by the Austrian economist constitute an excellent example of how a logician, starting from wrong axioms, can reach mathematically coherent but economically absurd conclusions.[13] Today we know the answer, which applies to the whole of standard economics, to Marshall's *memento*: mathematics has taken over.

Of course, we do not claim that the dominant economic theory is 'stupid', but rather consider that if a logically consistent theoretical construction arrives at paradoxical outcomes, then this is due to a series of fundamental axioms which, with the passing of time and models, are no longer remembered. Therefore, it would be worth questioning their content to be considered as a valid knowledge base. Unprovable axiomatic assumptions, especially the most critical and paradoxical ones, should be replaced by falsifiable hypothetical assumptions (Box 12). The current approach, on the other hand, builds on

[12] This quote can be found in the Preface of the *Principles* in the last four editions.

[13] Mathematics is a formally consistent method. A theorem correctly states that if you start from given a hypothesis you reach consistent conclusions. We should not be surprised that starting from false assumptions leads to far-fetched (such as the paradox of expansive austerity) and wrong conclusions: 'The problem arises from the fact that often the hypotheses are false, but well hidden and not easy to identify, and that the results, also false, are boasted as true as a consequence of a theorem' (Parisi, 2021: 82; our translation).

often precarious foundations which it attempts to consolidate by lengthening the 'chains of logic' and gradually becoming less robust.

In all of this, the problem is not the mathematics, but the choice of appropriate mathematics and then, the use made of it:

> Mathematics is a language that allows us to see complex relationships – or sometimes simple but extremely subtle relationships – with a clarity that we would not otherwise have. Good mathematical models take uncertainty into account. Problems do not depend on mathematics, but on those who use it wrongly. Think of the neo-liberal model – rather simplistic – or even other apparently more sophisticated models such as the DSGE, used by many economists and some central banks. The issue is not their mathematical formulation but the absurd assumptions they include. And in the fact that some policy-makers take these models more seriously than they deserve.[14]

Also, it should not be overlooked that classical physics, which inspired economics, can afford to adopt the reductionist principle because the system is separable, but this is not so valid for economics, which is a complex system made up of interdependent parts. Thus, it cannot be assumed that if the parts behave optimally the aggregate will do so too (thanks to the invisible hand). Much less is the opposite scenario valid because it becomes implausible to conceive of a collective rationality that is transferred to individuals (rational expectations). In fact, this hypothesis requires that there is no interaction and that it is possible to have the ideal construction of the representative agent (Box 5).

The motion of planets can be 'pen and paper' predicted millions of years in advance, just as it is 'easy' to guide a spacecraft millions of kilometres away. The rules remain the same because they are dictated by nature and do not change with the 'will' of the agents. The 'actions' and beliefs of astronomers do not influence the movements of the planets: one can publish an article on the orbit of Venus and Venus will continue its motion without having to take this into account. The same applies to atoms or sub-atomic particles. Conversely, an economist who publishes an article claiming that a more flexible labour market is conducive to economic growth can influence the course of the economy and people's lives, if some politicians were to believe him. The laws of physics, until proven otherwise, are stable although never definitive; the 'laws' of economics are reflexive and can be influenced by our beliefs about such laws.[15] As Morgenstern (1972; p. 707) explains:

[14] Gianrico Carofiglio interview to Joseph Stiglitz, 7th April, 2020, for *Gulliver*; our translation.

[15] Reflexivity in economics is the theory for which there is a feedback loop in which investors' perceptions influence economic fundamentals, which in turn changes investors' perceptions. More on reflexivity can be found in Soros (2013).

Box 5 Fallacy of Composition and the Representative Agent

The fallacy of composition is a mistake of interpretation one makes when assuming that what holds true for a system's constituent holds also true for the system. The fallacy of division is a mistake of interpretation one makes when assuming that what holds true for the system holds also true for all its parts.

If a system is populated by many heterogeneous and interacting individual agents, embedded into a multilevel hierarchy of network relationships, then it is complex. As such, the complex system is non-separable and non-reducible (Box 7), and it performs emergent phenomena that cannot be explained on the basis of the knowledge of individuals' behaviour, so it therefore takes a holistic (Box 2) perspective. In this case, assuming a reductionistic approach is like assuming the system is separable and reducible, 'as if' its behaviour could be explained by composition of its parts' behaviour, hence it is like forcing what is complex to behave 'as if' it were non-complex.

Reducing a complex system to a set of equivalently representative and separated parts is a seductive simplification, as it allows us to model one single part not to represent them 'all', but to represent them as a 'whole'. It is like the whole households' sector were behaving like a household to such an extent that modelling a household would be equivalent to modelling the whole households' sector. The fallacy of composition happens when one assumes that the behaviours of any of a complex system's parts also hold true for the whole system. This kind of composition is fallacious because a complex system is characterised by emergent phenomena that do not have equivalent counterparts in any of its parts: an emergent phenomenon pertains the system and it emerges from the bottom up by composition of heterogeneous and interacting parts' behaviour.

Kirman (1992; pp. 124–125) nicely illustrates the problem. Assume two consumers, a and b, with Cobb–Douglas preferences facing the same budget constraint (solid and dashed indifference curves respectively). Under the budget constrain **AE** they choose $\boldsymbol{y}_a$ and $\boldsymbol{y}_b$. Under **BD** they choose $\boldsymbol{x}_a$ and $\boldsymbol{x}_b$. Their aggregate choices are given by $\boldsymbol{y}_a + \boldsymbol{y}_b = \boldsymbol{y}$ lying on aggregate budget constraint **BF**, and $\boldsymbol{x}_a + \boldsymbol{x}_b = \boldsymbol{x}$ lying on **CE**.

Therefore, the 'representative individual' prefers $\boldsymbol{y}$ to $\boldsymbol{x}$, while agent a prefers $\boldsymbol{x}_a$ to $\boldsymbol{y}_a$ and agent b prefers $\boldsymbol{x}_b$ to $\boldsymbol{y}_b$, Hence, it is possible that the representative agent prefers a situation $\boldsymbol{y}$ over a situation $\boldsymbol{x}$, whereas all the individual 'represented agents' strictly prefer $\boldsymbol{x}$ over $\boldsymbol{y}$. 'Thus, to infer society's preferences from those of the representative individual, and to use these to make policy choices, is illegitimate' Kirman (1992; pp. 124–125).

Box 5 (Cont.)

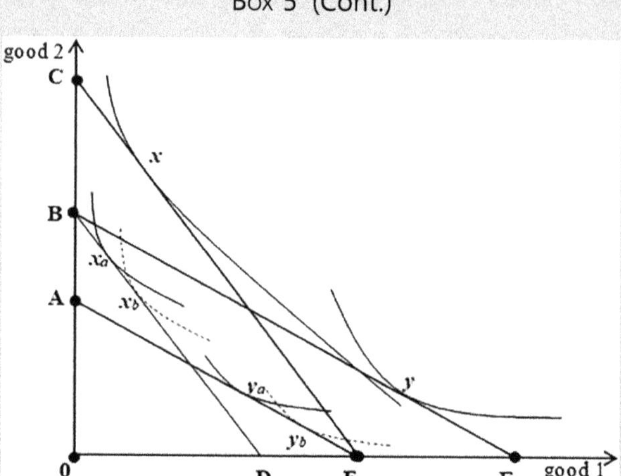

Figure 1 Fallacy of composition and the representative agent, adapted from Kirman (1992)

In economics the fallacy of composition is a widely diffused theoretical mistake that induces logical inconsistencies and incorrect modelling. It is made whenever one models a sector 'as if' it were an individual – say, a representative individual of the sector – and this is due to the methodological individualism approach. Even though in the economics literature there is no agreed definition about the representative agent (RA), it is nonetheless a widely used notion. *The Representative Agent in Macroeconomics*, by James E. Hartley (1997), analyses both theoretical and analytic aspects of the methodology. The 'critique' of Lucas (1976) warns that policy prescriptions based on macroeconomic models cannot grasp individual future behaviours, hence 'macroeconomic' laws should change accordingly or should be prepared on a micro-foundation ground that can be introduced by means of the representative agent argument. Although first introduced by Edgeworth (1881) and Marshall (1890), it is after the Lucas critique that RA became a cornerstone of the *mainstream* theoretical framework and modelling, but it lacks a secure ontological definition. It may be either a sort of 'average' agent or an agent that is mysteriously representative of the wider social group or class: say, the RA is the typical agent whose decisions are fairly good approximations of the 'average' decisions of most of the other agents. The RA may also be assumed as representative of the largest and most sufficiently homogenous group to such an extent that passing from the modelling of its behaviour to that of a system is but a matter of scaling. In any case, in adopting such a

Box 5 (Cont.)

reductionistic approach one models the economy complex system 'as if' it were separable and reducible (i.e., a non-complex system) while patently choosing not to consider the multiplicity of smaller parts in the system. Clearly this approach annihilates heterogeneity, although observable, and over-simplifies interaction, often reduced to a sort of indirect interaction, while many kinds of direct interactions among agents exist. To overcome a critique of homogeneity, and with the apparent ambition to explain the world as it is, in models one often involves two or more kinds of RA of the same type: say, poor and rich households; small-, medium-, and large firms; and so on. However, none of such RA is enough to model something like income distribution over the real, wide spectrum of incomes. Therefore, if the RA approach does not really represent a sufficient multiplicity of behaviours, any policy prescription is doomed to fail in improving societies' well-being. In the words of Kirman (1992; p. 119), 'the "representative" agent deserves a decent burial, as an approach to economic analysis that is not only primitive, but fundamentally erroneous'. Gallegati (1994) proves that heterogeneity, due to the asymmetric information of bankruptcy-adverse firms, give rise to composition effects that explain fluctuations and make the RA hypothesis false. Standard econometrics models are based upon the RA, which is a non-neutral assumption in this field too: as shown by Forni and Lippi (1997), econometric results in the analysis of the relation between aggregate consumption and income depend on the assumption of linearity and the absence of heterogeneity.

> Nature does not care … whether we penetrate her secrets and establish successful theories about her workings and apply these theories successfully in predictions. In the social sciences, the matter is more complicated and in the following fact lies one of the fundamental differences between these two types of theories: the kind of economic theory that is known to the participant in the economy has an effect on the economy … There is thus a 'back-coupling' or 'feedback' between the theory and the object of the theory, an interrelation which is definitely lacking in the natural sciences … In this area are great methodological problems worthy of careful analysis.

The social scientists live in the society they study, and their theories may influence its functioning and the feedback between the theory and the object of the theory that has no counterpart in the natural sciences.

In economics, the context or structure is constantly changed by innovations. No one can really believe that the same shock will produce the same effects in structurally different economies. We are in an uncertain world that does not respond to statistics. It is as if we were rolling a dice that has six sides and during the roll the number of sides changes, making any prediction impossible. From being complicated, the game becomes complex because new circumstances and actors emerge who, like those that preceded them, will interact and coordinate, modifying the structure. We have taken classical physics as a model and applied it to an object that is not relevant because it is characterised by emergence and structural evolution over time. The problem cannot be solved analytically if innovations change the boundary conditions. Since a differential equation admits infinite solutions, conditions must be set to find a particular one. In economics, this would be tantamount to assuming that there are no innovations and that the history of facts and ideas does not matter because everything is given at the beginning (Thurner et al., 2018).

After the Great Moderation, and perhaps also because of it, from the second half of the 1990s onwards the debate among economists came to a halt, to the extent that Lucas was able to say in 2003, in his farewell speech as President of the *American Economic Association*, 'My thesis in this lecture is that macroeconomics in this original sense has succeeded: Its central problem of depression prevention has been solved, for all practical purposes, and has in fact been solved for many decades' (Lucas, 2003, p. 1). Even then Lucas's words seemed out of place given the banking crisis in Sweden in the early 1990s, and the Asian financial crises of 1997–1998, and later in Russia, Brazil, and Argentina. Economic theory obviously reacts to the crisis. On the one hand, a sense of déjà vu: enriching the model by introducing first the banks and then the financial system, along with various rigidities, up to weak heterogeneity without questioning its axiomatic core, in a way that closely resembles the 'epicyclization' of the Ptolemaic system. On the other hand, while acknowledging its limitations, the theory is moderately open to new approaches, if it preserves the adoption of the neoclassical core, the 'scarcity paradigm', for which the prices of goods depend on their scarcity, and thus the equilibrium methodology. Trichet (2010) complains about the inadequacy of economic and financial models: 'As a policy-maker during the crisis, I found the available models of limited help. In fact, I would go further: in the face of the crisis, we felt abandoned by conventional tools.'[16] The real problem is not so much that the mainstream did not foresee the crisis, it is that in its models the possibility of having a crisis is not contemplated.[17]

---

[16] www.ecb.europa.eu/press/key/date/2010/html/sp101118.en.html.

[17] Parisi (1999) reminds us that: 'There have been three revolutions in physics [that] have changed the meaning of the word prediction. They are: (1) The introduction of statistical mechanics and of the first probabilistic reasoning by Maxwell, Boltzmann and Gibbs in the second half of the last century. (2) The discovery of quantum mechanics at the beginning of this century. (3) The study

But why, despite theoretical inconsistencies and empirical failures, does this kind of theory survive? Despite the fact that for Lucas (1980, p. 709) the objective was to build 'a FORTAN program that will accept specific economic policy rules as "inputs" and generate as "output" statistics describing the operating characteristics of time series we care about, which are predicted to result from these policies', economic theorists are highly reluctant to learn a general programming language that is powerful enough to undertake scientifically interesting computer modelling and testing of real-world economic systems. Hence, this reluctance is passed down from one 'generation' of economists to the next, along with self-protective disdain for those who do acquire and use such training. We cannot give ourselves any other answer: it happens by faith, because *mainstream* economics is reduced to a game of more intellectual than practical utility. Keynes (1936; appendix to chp. 14) reminds us that the same happened with the Ricardian system: 'Ricardo offers us the supreme intellectual achievement, unattainable by weaker spirits, of adopting a hypothetical world remote from experience as though it were the world of experience and then living in it consistently. With most of his successors common sense cannot help breaking in – with injury to their logical consistency.' Moreover, Keynes (1936; chp. 3) writes that

> The completeness of the Ricardian victory is something of a curiosity and a mystery. It must have been due to a complex of suitabilities in the doctrine to the environment into which it was projected. That it reached conclusions quite different from what the ordinary uninstructed person would expect, added, I suppose, to its intellectual prestige. That its teaching, translated into practice, was austere and often unpalatable, lent it virtue. That it was adapted to carry a vast and consistent logical superstructure, gave it beauty. That it could explain much social injustice and apparent cruelty as an inevitable incident in the scheme of progress, and the attempt to change such things as likely on the whole to do more harm than good, commended it to authority. That it afforded a measure of justification to the free activities of the individual capitalist, attracted to it the support of the dominant social force behind authority.

The two welfare theorems enunciated by Pareto provide the rigorous demonstration of the view that the market is desirable: 'It is not an overstatement to say that they are the underpinning of Western capitalism' (Fisher, 2013; p. 35). Because these are derived from general economic equilibrium theory, they form

of complex systems and the related techniques that have been developed in these last years. As an effect of these revolutions, the word prediction acquired a weaker meaning. Predictions in the context of the new paradigm are not acceptable with the old one (and sometimes the supporters of the old point of view try to deny to them a scientific validity). The positive consequence of the process is that the scope of physics becomes much larger and the constructions of physics find many more applications.'

the theoretical foundation according to which capitalism guarantees efficiency and optimality. By demonstrating that individual self-interest leads to collective welfare through the free market, one ensures one's own academic perpetuation, as if economics were a natural science, however scientifically unfounded, and not a discipline in which historical events matter.

As we propose, it is sufficient to limit oneself to take up the observations made, almost always formulated in theorems, by the neoclassical economists themselves as to why the standard model is logically wrong. There are still open problems, such as those arising from the impossibility of measuring aggregate capital (Sraffa, 1960; Garegnani, 1970), the implications arising from the 'anything is possible theorem' (Mas-Colell et al., 1995), the non-micro-foundable aggregation of the Cobb–Douglas production function, the Greenwald and Stiglitz (1986) theorem whereby imperfections of any kind generate Pareto improvable outcomes, the Boldrin and Montrucchio (1986) theorem against the uniqueness of the optimal equilibrium path, and Hahn's (1982) problem that there is no place for money in general equilibrium models that undermine the coherence of *mainstream* models and can no longer be swept under the carpet. They are all logical contradictions of a model that suggests a 'one size fits all' policy, also thanks to the slavish application of the 'Ricardian vice'.[18] It is no coincidence that at the first conference on complexity at the Santa Fe Institute the recurring question put to the economists by all the other participants (Waldrop, 1993) was 'do you really believe this?' They referred to the 'standard model' and its far-fetched assumptions, pointing to the need for a change in the economic paradigm towards complexity.

About paradigm shifts, let us summarise what has been said so far. In a non-separable system, none of its components can be analysed independently of the other: they are all part of a network that connects them in various ways. In contrast, the properties of a separable system are additive: the effect of a set of elements is the sum of the effects considered separately, and no new properties appear in the set that are not already present in the individual elements. If there are combined terms which depend on each other, then the aggregate is different from the sum of the parts, new effects appear, and innovations create them. In economics, methodological individualism is taken as valid, mathematical models are prepared which describe the system as if it were separable, and mathematical rigour based on axioms is preferred to empirical value. Typical of complex systems, such as economic ones, are the concepts of self-organisation and emergent behaviour. One of the consequences of self-organisation is that

[18] The 'Ricardian vice' refers to the construction of abstract models made of mathematical formulas with unrealistic assumptions. In simpler terms, it is the tendency of economists to formulate and test theories that are not troubled by the complexity of reality, resulting in theories that are mathematically beautiful but largely useless for practical applications.

one can no longer speak of universal laws, but only of stylised facts. Self-organisation and/or natural selection processes result in emergent and/or evolved behaviours. This will be the subject of the next section.

2 Economic Complex Systems

I think the next century will be the century of complexity.

Steven W. Hawking[19]

In the previous section we saw that mathematics is not a tool for the algebraic calculation of economic reasoning expressed in the form of equations; rather, it is the founding element of economic analysis itself, which wants to acquire a status as scientific on a par with physics. Although classical thought considered it unsuitable for such an approach because of its historical and social elements, the mathematical method in economic reasoning rapidly spread and transformed the discipline. Until 1870, economics dealt with large aggregates, but the marginalist revolution brought a radical change, and not only in methodology. The focus of analysis shifted from aggregates to individuals, from macro to economic micro-analysis. Mathematical tools are used that are designed for stable and complicated systems (for which equilibrium analysis is appropriate) but which are not suitable for analysing complex systems (whose equilibrium is statistical). The notion of statistical equilibrium (Box 6), in which the aggregate equilibrium is compatible with individual disequilibrium, is outside the box of tools of the *mainstream* economist (biologists say that an organism is in equilibrium only when it is dead). The equilibrium of a system no longer requires that every single element be in equilibrium by itself, but rather that the statistical distributions describing aggregate phenomena be stable – that is, in 'a state of macroscopic equilibrium maintained by a large number of transitions in opposite directions' (Feller, 1957, p. 356).

With the marginalist revolution, political economy becomes an oxymoron that dissolves into economics.

2.1 Defining Complexity is Complicated

The attribute 'complex' comes from Latin 'complector', meaning 'embracing'; therefore, complex is what embraces, what holds together. Rosser (2021) reminds us that complexity is a science in the making, not yet well identified, such that there are at least forty-five different definitions of complexity. In the literature there is no known definition of a complex system on which there is universal agreement, but there is good agreement that any definition involving

[19] Interview with San Jose, *Mercury News*, January 2000.

the key notions isolated here may be adequate. To summarise, we can isolate some key notions: heterogeneity, interaction, connectivity, irreducibility, non-separability, evolution, and emergence (see also Castañeda, 2021, 2022).

In this Element, we understand a complex system to be one that is composed of different parts that, compared to the macroscopic whole, are more elementary along a scale of 'granularity' that crosses different mesoscopic levels, until reaching the microscopic level, where the parts are no longer further decomposable.

Also, a system is complex if its structure and behaviour cannot be predicted from knowledge of all the constituents of the system. In terms of structural evolution, a complex system is characterised by 'emergent phenomena': events such that the behaviour and structure of the whole cannot be traced back to the behaviour and structure of any of its parts specifically, but to all of them 'together'. Therefore, while the behaviour and structure of a complicated system can be interpreted from the behaviour of all its components, and we do not expect any surprises, the same is not true for a complex system, which can instead give rise to 'emerging phenomena': facts that we observe at the different hierarchical levels, and that emerge from the network of the heterogeneous parts because of their interaction.

Box 6 Statistical Equilibrium

An economy is populated by many heterogeneous interacting agents that react to the ecology they create. They might be optimising agents or bounded rational agents, but this is irrelevant to an understanding of the system's behaviour (Aoki and Yoshikawa, 2006). The high degree of heterogeneity requires microeconomic behaviours to be stochastically conceived, and it asks for methods of statistical physics to approach equilibrium macroscopic properties of large numbers of interacting degrees of freedom – that is, when the system is complex (Kardar, 2007; p. ix). As Kubo et al. (1985; p. iv) taught us:

> The construction of macroscopic from microscopic elements on the basis of analyzed elements at the microscopic level is not limited only to physics. Macrosystems are synthesized from microscopic structure and dynamics in biology, the social sciences, psychology and other sciences as well. The activity of synthesizing is undoubtedly one of the most powerful methods of science. However, we may say that it is best organized and best developed in physics. This is, of course, because the objects studied in physics are simpler and more concrete than those of in other sciences, and theories can be more easily tested by means of experiments.

Assuming a statistical physics perspective leads to the notion of statistical equilibrium, that is a distribution pertaining the system itself as an

Box 6 (Cont.)

emergent phenomenon. In physics, a (isolated) system is said to be *in* statistical equilibrium if the system's observables over their subsystems assume values close to their expected values (Landau and Lifshitz 1980; p. 20). A complex system is *at* the statistical equilibrium even though its parts are not, such that, due to continuous interactions, jumps between equilibria happen due to endogenous forces that grow from the bottom up. The difference is summarised by Katz (2016, p. 6) as follows:

> A physical system only has to do one thing – 'be'- it doesn't make choices and it is constrained by physical laws to find a state of least energy or action. A biological/social system has to make choices consistent with the restrictions imposed by the laws of physics. A complex physical system evolves solely in state space while a complex biological/social system evolves in spaces of state and strategy allowing it to adapt.

Statistical equilibrium is a temporary state of compatibility among the system's parts and jumps may happen at different time lengths that depend on the contextual conditions that change with time, and this fact rules out ergodicity (Box 4). At different times the system can be in disequilibrium or in incomplete equilibrium, whereby only some subsystems can be in a compatibility state but not all. This aspect means that even if we conceive of the system as a whole, its components can behave differently: some of them may reach a state of compatibility before others, but only when they all do is the system at statistical equilibrium.

In statistical equilibrium theory, the market is seen as a system of prices, ruling economic units' interactions or transactions, defined over a probability space. In this way the market representation takes care of fluctuations and transaction-expected values, because of endogenous stochasticity, emerging from the micro-level and characterising macroscopic observables. As a matter of fact, there is not really a need for units to be in equilibrium with one another; only subsystems' conditions matter (Foley, 2003). Finally, being a temporary condition developing on agents' expectations before transactions, by their results in the environment agents are forced to revise their expectations. This mechanism of revision in expectations triggers a prices formation process which leads to subsequent equilibria. For further readings about statistical equilibrium in economics, see Foley (1994, 1996), Bargigli et al. (2013), and the literature cited therein.

Complexity economics is therefore the study of economies as complex systems, composed of interacting agents who adapt and change their actions according to the ecology they collectively contributed to determining (Arthur, 2013). Unlike *mainstream* economists who use individual optimisation and equilibrium methods, complexity economists deal with the emergence of stylised facts. On this basis, Arthur (2013) argues that non-equilibrium is the typical state of the economy, which is always in a state of flux, constantly evolving and changing (Dosi, 2023). In complexity economics, equilibrium is no longer defined by analogy with the classical physics perspective of a point at which opposite forces balance each other – say, just like the case of demand and supply. Complexity economics' equilibrium follows a probabilistic interpretation, more in analogy with statistical physics, thus leading to the notion of statistical equilibrium (Box 6).

From the relationship between information and innovation, we derive the concept of uncertainty noted in Section 1, which was introduced into economics by Knight (1921) and Keynes (1921). If all possible future events or the consequences of a decision are probabilistically calculable, the risk is Bayesian and the data-generating process (DGP) is ergodic (i.e., we can calculate the probability that an event will materialise). However, in complexity we cannot know all possible outcomes: in these situations of uncertainty, the calculation of probabilities has no solid foundation. Since there is no basis for any kind of uncertainty calculation, complexity theory assumes that economic agents try to solve this problem by guessing, using experience and simple decision heuristics ('rules of thumb'). They also constantly confirm or replace their strategies based on experience as agents explore, learn, and adapt.

Technological innovation is the other important element that determines the 'continuous becoming' of the economic system. Innovation is not just a one-off interruption of the equilibrium, but a generator of new technologies (Dosi, 1982) and structural transformations of the economy, wherein disequilibrium and metastability are conditions for temporary states of calm.

Thus, if one interprets the economy as a closed system, then stability can be approximated by equilibrium, while the presence of uncertainty and technological innovations means that economic systems are not in equilibrium. Moreover, meta-stable states are often multiple (due to feedback and increasing returns) and path-dependent (from previous states), and they can be chaotic and regularly go through phase transitions to end up in a different state from the starting one. If the system is in a steady state characterised by a strong resilience to change, it takes considerable shocks to move to another regime ('lock-in'; Arthur, 1989). If the resilience of a system is low, it could suddenly change its behaviour by switching to another regime by an endogenous process (Delli

Gatti et al., 1994). To study these dynamics adequately, complexity economics uses a broader set of tools than those of traditional economics.

The dominant economic theory is still using the mathematics of the eighteenth–nineteenth centuries to analyse complex systems 'as if' they were more like complicated mechanisms, while the hard sciences are continually updating their methods. The problem is not that 'old' mathematics is being used, but rather that it is inappropriate for interpreting the economy, which is a complex and unpredictable system. Complexity theory puts an end to the age of certainty. If agents interact directly then dynamic networks are formed, whose characteristics influence the characteristics of the stationary states. The theory of systems in equilibrium assumes that the dynamics of the system visits with the same probability all areas of phase space, regardless of the path followed. History is irrelevant and, therefore, the ergodicity hypothesis (Box 4) is assumed to be valid. On the contrary, since complex systems can be interpreted in probabilistic terms, complexity theory adopts the tools of modern statistical physics.

In economics, development and evolution depend on the specific history of systems, and since their components learn from experience, these systems can be regarded as complex adaptive systems (CAS). A non-linear dynamic system, even a deterministic one, can be completely unpredictable, at least in the usual interpretation of forecasting. Complexity is not used to predict how many millimetres of rain will fall tomorrow, but rather to estimate with what probability, and under what conditions, n millimetres of rain will fall tomorrow rather than m. Uncertainty, understood as non-deterministic predictability, is an intrinsic property of complex systems because they are non-separable (Box 7).

2.2 Reasoning about Economics is Complex

On the strength of mathematical formalism, *mainstream* theory has acquired a 'dominant position' and does not feel the need to implement a change of paradigm, but prefers to invest in mathematical-statistical techniques, with the ambition of providing descriptions of facts that are plausible and logically consistent. It prefers the 'reasoning in mathematics' in formal terms to the complex 'reasoning in economics' in analytical terms. The formalistic approach is powerful, but it requires such an abstraction that the economic problem is reduced to a pure mathematical problem (Blaug, 2003).

When economic reality does not obey the far-fetched but necessary assumptions, one treats the matter as a puzzle rather than a falsification of theory (Box 12). The model of perfect competition, populated by agents more akin to Laplace's demons (Laplace, 2007) than to human beings, is no more likely to explain reality than a haruspex. This is why general

Box 7 Separable and Non-Separable Systems

The importance of the granularity description depends on the phenomenon under study. From the macroscopic point of view, the system is a 'whole' of mesoscopic subsystems, each of which is composed of several microscopic entities, which we call elementary when they are no longer meaningfully fragmentable. Transferring the discourse to economics, an economic system is a macroscopic 'body', composed of subsystems, each of which is composed of more elementary parts until it reaches the scale of the single agent that is no longer decomposable into meaningful parts, so we consider it as the elementary constituent.

The systems of physics can be roughly divided into two broad categories: 'classical' and 'non-classical'. Non-classical systems are all those systems that can be described according to the principles of relativistic or quantum physics, as studied before the end of the nineteenth and beginning of the twentieth century in the works of Bohr, Planck, and Einstein. All the others are classical systems, and at least three characteristics are common to them: determinism, continuity, and separability.

A system is deterministic if it can be described by means of differential equations which, under given initial conditions – or even on the boundary conditions if partial derivative differential equations are required – make it possible to unambiguously predict the future from the present, albeit with some approximation due to the impossibility of measuring with absolute precision all the variables that define the spatiotemporally located state.

The continuity of a system refers to the fact that its evolutionary trajectories are continuous. In other words, the state space that can be visited by the system is everywhere dense and the passage from one state to another occurs with a succession of intermediate steps between indefinitely close states for indefinitely short time intervals.

A system is said to be separable if the properties of the whole depend on the contribution of the properties of its parts, which can each be described independently of the others, composed by algebraic summation. In some contexts, a separable system is considered to be linear, meaning that the properties of the whole are a linear combination of the properties of the parts (i.e., a weighted summation of them). Separability allows any part to be considered as representative of the whole, so that to describe the whole it is enough to describe one part of it, the rest being due to a scaling factor. Separability is thus the characteristic that makes a classical system reducible (Box 2). A separable system is therefore describable by the additive aggregation of the properties of its independent parts.

Box 7 (Cont.)

If this operation of aggregating properties is only possible in numerical terms, but not also in terms of the functions describing those properties, then we are dealing with a non-separable system. Under these conditions, however much determinism and continuity may apply, the mere fact that separability cannot be considered does not necessarily imply that the system is non-classical. For example, consider the prey–predator systems such as the Lotka–Volterra model. This model is deterministic and continuous, but it is not separable – we might even consider it non-linear in the sense mentioned earlier – because there is an indispensable mutual interdependence between prey and predators: it does not matter that the equations (the system as a mathematical entity) are analytically non-linear in mathematical terms; what matters is the interdependence that makes prey and predators inseparable. We cannot specify an equation for prey and one for predators in a decoupled way and think we can describe the ecosystem because prey and predators interact: predators eat prey for their subsistence, therefore without prey predators would become extinct, just as without predators, prey would take over. So, more than the mathematical non-linearity of the functions describing the parts, the message is that the interaction between heterogeneous parts is responsible for complexity.

According to this principle, the linearity or non-linearity of the equations of the system as a 'mathematical entity' is not the distinguishing or characterising element of a complex system as a 'physical entity'. The basis of complexity is always heterogeneity and interaction, hence non-separability and connectivity. A system is separable if the structural evolution of the whole is deductible, barring a scaling factor, from the structural evolution of any of its independent parts, otherwise the system is non-separable. Thus, for separable systems we can adopt the reductionist paradigm of the whole to some of its parts; for non-separable systems, the paradigm is holistic because they are complex.

equilibrium models are increasingly being enriched with limitedly rational and heterogeneous agents.

The hypothesis of a *homo œconomicus* – the idealised, perfectly rational, informed agent – is at odds with empirical studies of experimental economics. Herbert Simon (1997) reminds us that it is not empirically evident that entrepreneurs and consumers in making decisions follow the utility-maximising principles required by the marginalists' models, partly because they do not have sufficient information, or the necessary computational skills. Thus, the models need to anticipate that agents are uncertain about the future and need to include the costs of obtaining information. These factors limit the ability of agents to make predictions. However, such additions are not harmless for the general equilibrium as price dynamics do not clear the market or lead to a stationary equilibrium. That rigorous mathematical approach that was to have decreed the success of economics, no longer a moral discipline but a science, has buried it because it has been misused.

Classical physics cannot be applied to complex systems. The use of the representative part does not work when the system is non-separable and composed of heterogeneous interacting parts in a network of connections. Since interaction is at the basis of the difference between microscopic and macroscopic systems, one cannot apply the methodology of classical physics of reductionism and equilibrium to complex systems.

Accepting the existence of an analogy between economics and classical physics is tantamount to accepting three founding principles: mechanicism, reductionism, and determinism. Reasoning 'as if' separability were valid, since the formulation of the 'laws' of economics takes place through maximum and minimum problems valid for separable systems, employs the wrong method to describe reality.

If there is evolution, the boundary condition, which considers the influence of the future on today's activities, changes.[20] But this is only the case if the innovations which induce structural dynamics are not there and the information is perfect:

> The common practice of solving a dynamic general equilibrium model of a (often competitive) market economy by solving an optimisation problem is evidence of the fatal confusion in the minds of much of the economics profession between shadow prices and market prices and between cross-sectional conditions that are integral to solving an optimisation problem and the long-term expectations that characterise the behaviour of decentralised asset markets. (Buiter, 2009)

In physics there are examples of theories that were mathematically correct, but of little relevance in explaining the facts because they started from erroneous hypotheses: these theories led to results that were contradicted by reality. Scientists, however, have the 'strange' habit of considering that if the theory disagrees with

[20] In this perspective, one forgets Rosen's (2012) studies on the theory of anticipation, which is not about predicting the future but creating the conditions today so that tomorrow we can make the right choices to achieve what we want after tomorrow. In Di Guilmi et al. (2017, chp. 5), together with those of reflexivity theory in Soros' (2013) interpretation, these principles are applied in the specification of an ABM model on financial fragility.

an experiment, then they reason about the hypotheses on which the model is based and identify which hypotheses are fragile to adopt better ones: hence, they change the model. Without renouncing mathematical rigour (consistency), empirical relevance is important, and the comparison with reality (correctness). The correctness of the model decrees its usefulness without renouncing its logical consistency.

The available methodologies and tools open the door to a different economy from the dominant one to consider observable phenomena such as behavioural imitation, interaction between heterogeneous agents, and historical time. The current approach, however, is axiomatic-deductive, disinterested in its formal limitations such as the fact that general equilibrium theory is subject to Gödel's incompleteness theorems (Box 8) and cannot generate empirically falsifiable propositions (Box 12).

Box 8 Kurt Gödel and the Incompleteness Theorem

Along with Aristotle, Kurt Gödel (1906–1978) is the greatest logician in history: various sources report that Einstein said he chose Princeton for the pleasure of walking to home with Gödel to talk. Gödel is famous for what is known as the incompleteness theorem, but this is composed of two distinct, albeit related, theorems that mark the limits of mathematics. The first statement of the theorem was given verbally by Gödel in 1930, at the congress on the fundamentals of mathematics in Köningsberg. After several talks, Gödel said:

> If we stick to these fail-safe methods there will always be true conjectures that cannot be proved and mathematical problems that can never be solved. We can adopt the safe methods of reasoning, but then there will be problems that we will not be able to solve. Or we may have the potential ability to solve all problems, but without the certainty of having solved them correctly. We will never be certain of the methods and at the same time have the ability to solve all the problems. (Piñero, 2014, pp. 11–12)

Let us now look at simplified versions of the Gödel theorems (Raatikainen, 2020).

G1. *Any consistent formal system, within which a certain amount of elementary arithmetic can be carried out, is incomplete: that is, there are statements of the language of the formal system which can neither be proved nor disproved in the formal system.*

G2. *For any consistent formal system, within which a certain amount of elementary arithmetic can be carried out, the consistency of the formal system cannot be proved in the formal system itself.*

We saw that *mainstream* economics descends from general economic equilibrium theory, an axiomatic mathematisation of economic thinking through the formal system of mathematical economics. Thus, as they mark the limits for mathematics, G1 and G2 also mark the limits for economics that has fallen into the coherence–incompleteness trap, from which it can escape only by opening its set of axioms to reality, to testable hypotheses. The theory of general economic equilibrium is subject to the Gödel incompleteness theorem. On the one hand, we will find problems that we cannot solve; on the other hand, we will not be able to prove that the solutions are appropriate, in the paradoxical condition of being able to find solutions that are formally consistent but empirically incorrect, and therefore of little practical use (Landini et al., 2020). Confusing the equilibrium of a decentralised market economy with the result of a mathematical programming exercise is not acceptable. Models incorporating the axiom of complete – hence, efficient – markets, under the illusion that they describe models of decentralised market economies, are in fact models of a centrally planned economy. The Walrasian auctioneer, who guarantees the right boundary conditions, is nothing more than the benevolent dictator in the guise of the central planner. On the other hand, information is partial, private, or asymmetrical; there is no other perspective than self-organisation and strategic behaviour.

Self-organisation is a spontaneous emergent phenomenon in complex systems; typically, far from a state of equilibrium, they make a transition to a more ordered state due to the composition of the effects of the decentralised behaviour of their constituents. A complex system is considered to exhibit self-organisation if it (a) is an open system, (b) is far from an equilibrium state, (c) its structural evolution is characterised by non-linear dynamics, and (d) there are feedback effects between its constituents and the structures being formed.

Strategic behaviour occurs between heterogeneous interacting agents and gives rise to a network, wherein the nodes are the agents and the links are the interactions. Walras' system is a star-shaped network with a central coordinator, who is fully informed, and agents who have no information about what the others are doing. If we remove the central node and give everyone free access to information, then the network becomes complete. Conversely, if information is expensive an information efficient market is impossible: the paradox of Grossman-Stiglitz (1980).

If this is the situation, then modern macroeconomics is in bad shape. But it is also to be expected that an increasing role will be played by behavioural approaches, which are based on empirical studies of how agents learn, form opinions about the future, and change these opinions in response to changes in their environment. The future of economics will be that of a complex and empirically based 'social science'. Tools such as rational expectations or heterogeneous but non-interacting agents will end up alongside epicycles as memories of failed theories, not because they are logically inconsistent but because they are incorrect.

Beyond this, one should also consider that the problem of micro-foundation in economics is badly posed. The attempt to explain macro-behaviour as a summation of individual behaviours has not achieved a satisfactory result because the topic is treated in a way that is improper and does not match reality (incorrectness). As Pietronero (1998) reminds us,

> the knowledge of the trajectories of all the atoms in a gas does not necessarily lead us to the concept of entropy or to the Boltzmann and Gibbs laws of thermodynamics. Understanding gas behaviour requires the introduction of new concepts that refer to the average properties of the system. These thermodynamic concepts have their own fundamental laws that can be related, but only remotely, to the laws of microscopic dynamics. (our translation)

If we transfer this similarity to the field of economics, the most appropriate methodology is that of agent-based modelling (ABM; Gallegati et al., 2024). When there is interaction between the elements, complex structures are formed that have different properties than those of the individual components in isolation. So, economics needs different tools than the usual ones. In economics, the role of history must also be considered and, moreover, historical time is irreversible. The events that have taken place, such as innovations or crises, can neither be cancelled nor refuted; at most they can be overcome but, in any case, they leave a trace that affects the evolution of economic systems.

But there is a further argument. Saying that 'history matters' simply means that 'the arrow of time' is not negligible either for the system as a whole or for its constituents. As Georgescu-Roegen (1970) taugt us, in economics there is nothing but money that can go back and forth between past and present; all the other items in the economic process follow a unidirectional route. Along with that (economic) process we call 'production', any kind of matter is transformed from a state of high disposable energy (precious resources) to a state of high non-disposable energy (useful manufacts), together with a significative amount of waste (not precious resources). At a higher, although intuitive, level of abstraction it can therefore be generally said that any kind of human activity leaves a trace in the course of history that cannot be neglected along with the course of human systems' evolution, which involves adaptation to states inherited from the past.

The Santa Fe Institute in New Mexico, founded in 1984 by Arrow, among others, is dedicated to the study of CAS, wherein agents can adapt and change behaviour as a result of experience. The ability to learn and to formulate differentiates economic agents from atoms. CAS are non-separable, self-organising systems composed of many interacting parts that give rise to emergent aggregate behaviour; adaptation is achieved through the continuous redefinition of relationships within the system and between the system and its environment (co-evolution).

In self-organising systems we observe 'scale invariant' phenomena (Box 9) and the spontaneous attainment of a state of statistical equilibrium (Box 7). As far as the system loses energy in self-organisation, we are therefore in the

Box 9 Scale Invariance

A quantity is said to be scale invariant if it is statistically similar at different levels of observation. Complex systems are not only made up of heterogeneous interacting parts through a structure of relational networks, but are also organised according to a structural hierarchy of these networks that goes from the micro-level, that of their elementary constituents, through one or more meso-levels, where the constituents organise themselves, to reach the macro-level of the system.

If the distribution of a given quantity preserves its statistical properties at different levels of scale (i.e., for different forms of observation units) that quantity is said to be scale invariant, whereby the scale is relative to the observation units. There is also another way to understand scale invariance in complex systems – namely, if the structure or the processes that are activated do not change the functional form of one or more quantities as the spatial or temporal scale changes.

If we can state that the quantity Y is a function of quantity X by means of the following expression $y = f(x)$, Y is scale invariant if the following dilatation holds: $f(s \cdot x) = g(s) \cdot f(x)$, where s is a constant. If we set $f(x) = a \cdot x^b$, where a and b are parameters peculiar of the phenomenon, then $f(s \cdot x) = a \cdot (s \cdot x)^b = s^b \cdot (a \cdot x^b) = s^b \cdot f(x)$, given that $g(s) = s^b$ it follows that $f(s \cdot x) = g(s) \cdot f(x)$, therefore s is interpretable as a scale factor. If $f(x)$ is the distribution of X, where is a realisation at a given unit of measure, $f(s \cdot x)$ is the distribution of X by a multiple or sub-multiple s of the original unit of measure: if $f(s \cdot x) = g(s) \cdot f(x)$ the distribution of X in the new scale is the same as the distribution with the original unit of measure

Box 9 (Cont.)

with a difference due to a multiplicative scale factor $g(s)$ that does not change the shape. As examples we may consider the Cobb–Douglas function $f(k,l) = A \cdot k^a \cdot l^b$ and the power law distribution $f(x) = a \cdot x^{-b}$: this last one was analysed earlier; just substitute b with $-b$, therefore let us see what happens with the Cobb–Douglas calculating $f(p \cdot k, q \cdot l) = A \cdot (p \cdot k)^a \cdot (q \cdot l)^b = (p^a \cdot q^b) \cdot A \cdot k^a \cdot l^b = g(p,q) \cdot f(k,l)$.

One of the markers of complexity is precisely the power law distribution. If the right tail of the distribution of a quantity, which is generated in the system because of interactions between heterogeneous agents, follows a power law, while its main body follows a different law – typical is the case of an exponential family law – this fact is an indicator that the system is complex but also that the quantity in question is characterised by scale invariance. Then there are more articulated situations in which the scale invariance is not observed in the right tail but within a precise subset of the realisations; in these cases the probabilistic model is said to be a power law with an exponential threshold.

An interesting aspect of scale invariance is that if a given quantity is scale invariant, any random sample of it will obey this property if the population and samples are large enough to validate this result in inferential terms.

In the current state of knowledge, the mechanism that generates this property is not yet well established. However, the greatest consensus on the genesis of this property concerns the typical characteristics of complexity, namely the heterogeneity and interaction that determine emergent phenomena. Katz (2016) provides a clear treatment of the topic, a review of scale invariant phenomena, an application, useful motivations for policy making, and, finally, a bibliography on the topic.

zone of dissipative and out-of-equilibrium systems: we must introduce new ideas and methods.

The concept of spontaneous generation of critical structures, also known as SOC (self-organised criticality; Box 10), is explored in detail in the sandpile models introduced by Bak et al. (1987). The random addition of sand grains leads the system towards a steady state – corresponding to a 34° inclination – and to the formation of avalanches, with a scale-invariant distribution, when the inclination is greater. Self-organised criticality emerges spontaneously. The ideas of self-organisation have been successfully adopted and have rapidly invaded the sciences by providing the means to understand scale invariance

Box 10 Self-Organised Criticality

Self-organised criticality is a complex system phenomenon tied to self-organisation and scale invariance (Box 9) firstly conceived by Bak et al. (1987) (but see also Ashby (1947), Bak et al. (1993, 1996), Brunk (2001), and Hoffman and Payton (2018)). Although the notion had been formally developed in physics it has also been introduced in economics: among others, see Sheinkman and Woodford (1994).

Well synthesised by Golyk, 'SOC is a property of dynamical systems to organize its microscopic behavior to be spatial (and/or temporal) scale independent', meaning that it is system evolution that organises itself into a complex structure with critical behaviour.[21] As a consequence, SOC is typical of non-equilibrium complex systems where complexity is revealed by power-tailed distributions that are scale invariant. All these notions have been successfully developed in complexity economics: see Arthur et al. (1997).

Although this phenomenon is reminiscent of the phase transitions, this is a *false-friend* image. Phase transitions – for instance, from liquid to gaseous state of matter – happen at given values of parameters, like pressure and temperature, that can be tuned or determined out of the system – say, exogenously: when both reach the so-called critical values, what was liquid becomes gaseous. On the contrary, as far as SOC is due to self-organisation, then it is due to the system behaviour from the inside – say, endogenously.

and complexity. In SOC models the dynamics are irreversible, meaning that systems with SOC are non-ergodic (Box 4).

2.3 Complexity Economics

According to Arthur (1999, p. 107),

> common to all studies on complexity are systems with multiple elements adapting or reaching to the pattern these elements create … Time enters naturally here via adjustment and change … Barring the reaching of some asymptotic state or equilibrium, complex systems are systems in process that constantly evolve and unfold over time … Such systems arise naturally in the economy … But, unlike ions and spin glass, which always react in a simple way to their local magnetic field, economic 'elements' – human agents – react with strategy and foresight by considering outcomes that might result as a consequence of behavior they might undertake.

[21] See www.mit.edu/~8.334/grades/projects/projects12/V.%20A.%20Golyk.pdf.

Economics should deal with reality as it is realised over time, as it could become, and investigate specific structures and processes of economic agents through the mechanism of evolution. Like biological systems, economic systems are conditioned by chains of historical events. Since the ability to learn from experience is fundamental, economics should be oriented towards the analysis of complex adaptive systems. Adaptation to the environment is reflected in the tendency towards equilibrium but, in economics, the environment evolves through the action of agents; it is constantly changing, and we therefore need new tools compared to those adopted so far. White (2023, p. 21) takes this point seriously and shows 'how a computer simulation of an agent-based model responds to disruptive events, in the context of an economic model'.

The concept of complexity has its roots in the nineteenth-century works of Henri Poincaré and became established in the last century. The principle of emergence removes any possible reductionism. The concepts of heterogeneity and interaction necessarily lead to the question of non-linearity and the

Box 11 The Notion of Emergence

Emergence is the property that characterises complex systems, distinguishing them from those that present themselves as complicated mechanisms (Johnson, 2006). Here, we will try to explore this topic on which philosophy, first, and science, later, have reasoned at least since the time of Aristotle. Without going so far back in time, one of the earliest arguments on the notion of emergence, which will form the basis of the modern interpretation of the concept, can be found in a much cited expression by John Stuart Mill (1843): 'To whatever degree we might imagine our knowledge of the properties of the several ingredients of a living body to be extended and perfected, it is certain that no mere summing up of separate actions of those elements will ever amount to the action of the living body itself' (p. 398). This argument explains that the behaviour of living entities, among which we can also include societies, involves the 'failure of aggregativity or linearity of influence among their elements' (O'Connor, 2021, p. 5).

O'Connor (2021) provides one of the most comprehensive treatments of the notion of emergent properties. In this contribution, the author devotes himself to three topics in particular: the analysis of ontological aspects, the definitions of weak and strong emergence, and their opposition.

From an ontological point of view, two main categories are considered: dependency and autonomy. Emergences depend on the micro-configurations

Box 11 (Cont.)

of the system in which they occur and are autonomous from these because the system and its parts are distinct entities. Dependence can be understood as modal, functional, and random. Modal dependence means that 'emergents modally depend on their physical bases, such that it is necessary that if an emergent occurs, some or other physical basis occurs, and it is further necessary that if that basis occurs the emergent occurs' (O'Connor (2021, p. 9). Autonomy comes in three perspectives: non-aggregativity, multiple realisability, and distinctive efficacy. Non-aggregativity consists in the impossibility or absence of certain properties such as associativity, commutativity, linearity and invariance by decomposition and regrouping (O'Connor, 2021, p. 12). Modal dependence and autonomy as non-aggregativity are the characteristics that we can find underlying the notion of emergence as understood in this Element.

In 2000, the *International Journal of Systems Studies* devoted a special issue to 'Emergent Properties of Complex Systems'. Amongst the various contributions, that of Damper (2000), from which we have drawn extensively, provides a summary of the main currents of thought only partially dealt with here, both in the philosophical and scientific fields, and which have found some convergence on the notion of emergence as we commonly understand it.

Alexander (1920) argues that 'higher' level properties emerge from those of parts in more 'fundamental' levels, although they do not characterise any of these, and that this must be accepted as a fact that can only be accepted without being able to be explained. An 'emergent' – be it a phenomenon, a property, or a quality of the system – is thus a systemic fact, but not all systemic facts are also emergent; only those that change the behaviour of the system that possesses them to such an extent that its internal processes cannot be traced back to the behavioural laws of their constituents are. All systemic facts that are not 'emergent' are 'resultants' – that is, facts that can be directly traced back to the composition of the behaviour of the constituents and for the understanding of which at the systemic level we can make use of the laws governing the most fundamental levels. Between 'emergent' and 'resultant' there is thus the same tension that we find between 'holism' and 'reductionism' (Box 2). In other words, just as the production value of an industry is the resultant of all the production values of the enterprises operating in it, the aggregate production function is an emergent of the individual production functions of the enterprises.

O'Connor (1994) explains that between 'radical dualism' and 'reductionism' an intermediate way has developed, according to which what is

Box 11 (Cont.)

'grounded in' and at the same time 'emergent from' a material structure (i.e., a hierarchical structure for different levels of subsystems, from the highest to the most fundamental) must be considered 'emergent', which makes it necessary to understand the micro–macro relations within a system.

Thus, an 'emergent' is a feature that pertains to the system rather than its parts; it cannot be predicted before its manifestation, nor can it be interpreted according to the rules or laws that govern the subsystems of the system's hierarchical structure at a more 'fundamental' level. In this extreme synthesis we find the idea of unpredictability according to Gell-Mann (1994): namely, that some behaviours of complex systems cannot be predicted from the behaviour of their constituents even when these follow very simple rules. According to Crick (1994), theoretically, and insofar as the whole is not the sum of its parts (Anderson, 1972), systemic behaviour could be understood if the behaviour of its parts and the way they interact were understood. Thus, underlying the notion of emergence we find the notion of 'systemic structure' (i.e., a hierarchy of subsystems that constitute the parts of the system at different levels) and 'interaction' (i.e., the interactive behaviour of the parts without any external coordination). Considering this 'dialogic' relationship between the different levels of the systemic structure, Anderson (1972) explains that natural phenomena emerge at a given level because of other phenomena that are activated on more 'fundamental' levels, and Holland (1990) adds that 'fundamental' phenomena constrain those on higher levels.

If Alexander (1920) argues that it is impossible to explain emergence beyond the factual, and Casti (1997) speaks of it in terms of unpredictable surprise, other authors nevertheless attempt to elaborate categories, analytical methods, or principles to make emergence more ontologically intelligible. These include Cariani (1991), who distinguishes computational, thermodynamic and model-related emergence; Steels (1991), who introduces the idea of emergent functionality; and Stephan (1998), who introduces three categories in order to distinguish what is emergent from what is not: non-reducible, non-predictable properties and weak emergence. The notion of weak emergence, as opposed to strong emergence, is introduced by Bedau (1997): weak emergence relates to those states of the system that can be understood from the microstates of their constituents by means of reductionist methods, which is closer to the notion of 'resultant' for Alexander, whereas strong emergence relates to those states of the system that condition behaviour at more fundamental levels, thus it is a notion closer to Alexander's notion of 'emergent'. See also Johonson (2006).

emergent behaviour of a system. But if elements are combined or self-organised, then there is interconnection between them through networks of relationships, and thus new effects emerge.

Although in nature and in the human sciences the relationships between the magnitudes of different phenomena are essentially non-linear, for a first approximation the assumption of linearity can be assumed to be valid. Unfortunately, mathematical models of economics limit themselves to this simplification and describe the system 'as if' it were linear, sometimes adopting linear approximations in the given contours of certain points of interest.

However, economic systems are non-separable and individual elements interact and self-organise; this makes it impossible to speak of universal laws, but only of specific 'laws' and emergent behaviour: there is no isomorphism between micro- and macro-behaviour.

Technological innovation, for example, changes the structure of the economy and thus the ecology of which companies and households are part. In mathematical language, innovations and new knowledge are equivalent to changes in the initial and boundary conditions, so that the state space that the system can visit is no longer fixed. Since, to solve the equations that describe the economy, according to the dominant approach, one needs stable boundary conditions, then any novelty that changes the environment and the dynamics cannot be considered, except as an 'impulse' that disrupts the trajectory and that must be controlled to 'respond' appropriately so as to return the dynamic to its original path.

Economics is a social science that analyses individual behaviour guided by incentives and information. The attempt to subsume economics into physics implies the reduction of *homo œconomicus* to the atom. If the theory were correct the future would be predictable. But this would imply that agents would have to behave mechanically in an optimal way, reacting passively rather than acting proactively. However, new physics has shown that this view cannot be applied in the presence of irreversible phenomena. Reductionism and equilibrium are applicable to a complicated and structurally stable mechanism, not to a complex system where the way agents interact may change over time. If an innovation occurs and is successfully introduced, then the ecology of the system and the information 'endowments' change, stimulating new forms of interaction.

Complexity emphasises that agents react to changes brought about by the actions of other agents and that there can be aggregate equilibrium and individual disequilibrium. Taking this into account complicates the concept of equilibrium, because it introduces variability that the general equilibrium

Box 12 Karl Popper and the Principle of Falsifiability

Philosopher of science Karl Popper introduced the principle of falsifiability to distinguish between controllable and uncontrollable theories. Controllable theories are those that can be confronted with reality to assess how accurately their deductions agree with the facts; the others are uncontrollable. Consequently, a theory is only scientific if it is falsifiable; if it is not, then it is not scientific. A corollary of this deduction is that, to paraphrase Einstein, no matter how much evidence one may adduce in support of a theory in order to consider it a valid basis of knowledge, a single instance of counterevidence is enough to refute it. Therefore, this implies that no scientific theory is to be considered definitively true, but any scientific theory can be considered a valid basis of knowledge, only until proven otherwise, provided it is falsifiable.

In purely logical terms (i.e., without making value judgements), the principle of falsifiability explains that from theoretical premises, such as first principles or axioms, it must be possible to derive an experiment which, if it fails, calls the whole theory into question, starting from its foundations.

model cannot cover. Statistical physics was developed to abandon the deterministic description for a probabilistic description, whose states are not determinable a priori.

When the system is complex it is not possible to associate an effect with a well-defined cause. The cause–effect investigation assumes separability, which does not hold when the aggregate is not the sum of its components but is a non-separable whole determined by their interaction. By focusing on systems in equilibrium, economists implicitly accept that the number of possible states can be understood and limited to the duration of the 'equilibrium'.

In the absence of stability, probabilistic evaluation of individual outcomes becomes very difficult. This point reflects the more pervasive and structural problem of non-linearity and emergence in complex systems. Brian Arthur has reasoned that the term 'non-equilibrium economics' would be more appropriate than 'complexity economics'. And, since equilibrium is a special case of non-equilibrium, traditional economics is a special case of complexity. Complexity sees the economy as an ever-changing phenomenon. Economic agents use different rules because the outcomes to which they must individually react are new. The resulting economy is an unpredictable evolving complex system that constantly rebuilds itself: strategies evolve, time becomes important, structures are formed, and emerging phenomena appear. Economic agents are constantly changing actions and strategies in response to the outcome they create by interacting. This further modifies the outcome, which requires them to react again. Agents therefore live in a world in which their beliefs, actions, and strategies are successively tested to survive within an 'ecology' that their behaviour simultaneously creates and destroys.

Complexity economics therefore asks how actions, strategies, and expectations can change endogenously with the patterns they help to create. Complexity economics can be read as an extension of equilibrium economics to non-equilibrium. And because equilibrium is contained in disequilibrium, complexity is more than a generalisation of *mainstream* theory: a new paradigm in economics is thus taking shape.

Complexity economists use a wide variety of theoretical and empirical methods on stylised facts: from machine learning to experimental evidence (Hommes 2013); from network analysis to power law research (Axtell, 2001; Gabaix 2009) to the study of Big Data; from statistical moment mapping (Cont 2001) to standard econometrics (Angrist and Pischke 2017). Complex, or non-equilibrium, dynamics allows for 'three steps' ahead of the empirical evidence that standard models can capture and allows for the explanation of stylised macro-facts along with meso- and micro-facts where ABM methodology is decidedly superior (see Gallegati et al., 2024). Many mathematical modelling techniques are used for the formalisation of complexity models: networks (Caldarelli et al., 2004), non-linear dynamics (Bischi et al., 2017), and ABM (Gallegati et al., 2017). These types of models are all capable of analysing non-equilibrium behaviour typical of open systems.

Complexity economics differs from the prevailing economic paradigm that makes equilibrium and optimisation the norm. It can be argued that the *mainstream* views the economy as a deterministic, highly predictable, and mechanistic system, whereas complexity economics is a process-dependent, organic, and ever-evolving organism. Equilibrium economics is a special case of non-equilibrium and thus of complexity economics (Arthur 2021). Since its formal models are almost always made to explain a set of observed phenomena or stylised facts, which can then in turn be used to inspire further empirical work, the methodological approach of complexity economists is more inductive.

For a new paradigm, where quantitative evidence is crucial and analytical consistency is not derived from axiomatic models, ABM is very promising, although still immature (Gallegati et al., 2024). Agent-based models aim to represent economic systems as evolutionary, adaptive, and complex systems, composed of heterogeneous and boundedly rational individuals interacting with each other, generating the emergent properties in the system itself. Thus, if the economy is complex, the appropriate methodology to analyse it integrates the ABMs and methods of complexity theory. The economic equilibrium – its uniqueness or multiplicity, stability or instability, crises and fluctuations – becomes only one of the possible outcomes of a model that integrates an observable phenomenology and is calibrated on real data, not the result of an axiom.

As discussed in Gallegati et al., (2024), with ABM the methodology is developed 'from the bottom up': individual parameters are estimated with experiments (Colasante, 2017) and econometric surveys (Bargigli, 2017), their statistical robustness – as a distribution – is assessed, and, finally, it is evaluated whether aggregate regularities emerge in agreement with the stylised facts. In short, there is micro-, meso-, and macro-empirical validation: within the limits of what is knowable, this makes a model that, in addition to the 'why' also answers the 'how', almost complete and coherent. Four centuries after Galileo, with ABM the falsification of theories is also applied to economics.

For example, we can set up an experiment involving a financial crisis like the one in 2007–2008 using the ABM method, which becomes the economist's laboratory. But if the ABM experiment reveals that the model is not correct, we have to go back to the equations and remove the uncorroborated ones. On this point, the ABM methodology is well prepared because it can implement hypotheses that have been previously found to be factual, while the DSGE method is less so, or not so at all, because it is anchored to axioms, which it accepts for what they are: unquestionable revealed truths.[22] On the basis of this, we can conclude that the dominant economy produces theories that cannot be falsified (Kirman, 1989), and therefore excludes itself from the scientific world which inspired it and which it can only enter by claiming its priorities of logical consistency and correctness.

3 Conclusion

Economics was formed in the 1870s according to the thinking of Stanley Jevons, Carl Menger, and Leon Walras, using classical physics as a model. To form the scientific status of economics, the insight of the neoclassicists was to transfer the ideas and mathematical apparatus of physics of the time into economics. The result was that the formalistic approach to economics did not care too much about 'reasoning about economics', preferring mathematical deduction. Thus, mainstream economists have ended up being more concerned

[22] Unlike the DSGE method, the ABM method is open to reality and does not require axioms but only testable hypotheses. Furthermore, while ABM can be applied to non-reducible systems, DSGE requires that the system be reducible.

with the characteristics of the states of an economy than with how those states are achieved.

According to the neoclassical interpretation, material points, representing systems of identical particles or macroscopic systems such as planets, become representative of economic entities such as individuals, enterprises, households, and consumers. Force is replaced by marginal utility and energy is considered equivalent to utility while the law of equilibrium is transferred from physics to economics. In classical physics, an equilibrium point is determined by the balancing of equal and opposite forces at the maximum of the net energy function, whereas in economics the equilibrium position is determined by the equality of supply and demand at the maximum of the objective function. Furthermore, the methodological basis analyses markets and economies as closed systems that try to reach a state of equilibrium. However, only in the case of reducible systems is this isomorphism possible – that is, only when the aggregate behaviour equals the sum of the individual ones, and thus without direct interaction between agents and non-linearity.

Non-linearity is understood as the effect of interaction and feedback between agents. If the feedback is positive, this determines what is called 'emergence' – that is, new facts that emerge through successive levels of aggregation and that are not predictable or explainable by the properties of the single elements at a lower level. On the other hand, if the feedback is negative, there is self-regulation.

The main characteristic of adaptive complex systems is emergence. Certain phenomena emerge as a result of the actual interaction between heterogeneous constituents and cannot be explained from given micro-rules, which are assumed to underlie individual behaviour and action. To observe the emergence of given phenomena, it is not usually sufficient to consider a minimal heterogeneity of a few different groups, but internally homogeneous to the point of being able to reduce them to representative agents, which do not actually interact, as happens in the HANK models. A system characterised by emergence is then said to be complex and deterministic cause–effect relations are thus definitively lost.

It should also be noted that, almost at the same time as the publication of the works of the leading marginalist economists, a great revolution took place in physics due to the concept of entropy and quantum analysis. There is no longer any room for the dream of extending the mechanistic and deterministic method of classical mechanics to economics; rather, the statistical analysis of elements and their aggregate behaviour is gaining ground. In short, economics was born old and unviable. With entropy, the idea that the arrow of time exists – that it is irreversible – and that there is no temporal symmetry (i.e., that it is impossible to return to the initial configurations) comes into the picture.[23] The social sciences do not obey determinism, and statistical physics, with its principle of indeterminacy, is more suitable than classical physics, which ignores the problem of entropy. In fact, the second principle of thermodynamics states that one cannot predict future states of a complex system; prediction is only possible for linear systems that admit equilibrium. On the contrary, a non-linear system is typically far from equilibrium and can admit more than one equilibrium.

According to Beinhocker (2006), the dynamics of economies cannot be characterised by a set of equilibrium conditions because they are evolutionary systems. For this same reason, biologists have not attempted to develop a theoretical framework to explain the functioning of an ant colony because of equilibrium. The integration of elements of statistical physics with features of evolutionary biology in the same paradigm poses the challenge of adapting the theoretical frameworks of each discipline. From physics it is important to consider that the interaction of agents produces collective behaviour that cannot be deduced directly from the behaviour of the parts. From biology it is worth pointing out that imitation and learning are essential aspects of the cognitive capacities of human beings (Gintis, 2006).[24]

The *liason dangerous* between economics and physics can be summarised as follows. If the economic system is not complex, then we can apply the tools of classical physics. However, if we recognise that the economic system is complex, then we must consider the tools of statistical physics. Since economic agents are not atoms but entities endowed with the capacity for learning and choice, then the problems arising from incomplete information cannot be overlooked. If the economic system is affected by innovations and these innovations change its structure, then we also move beyond the idea of complexity in physics into the field of statistical biology.

The relationship between economics and physics is very dangerous, especially when it neglects the relevance of time, ignores interactions describing an ergodic system, and forgets that the former is a social science while the latter is a natural science. Over the past 150 years, several revolutionary discoveries in physics have been ignored by *mainstream* economics because they undermine traditional economic knowledge.

[23] In *On the Value of Statistical Laws in Physics and the Social Sciences* (2006), Majorana points out that individuals in a society are not the equivalent of atoms because human beings are endowed with free will and can make voluntary, sometimes wrong, choices.

[24] Rosser (2021) recalls, how from Veblen derives the possibility of a complex emergence of higher orders of institutions based on cooperation like the theory of multilevel evolution developed by biologists such as Crow (1955), Hamilton (1964), and Price (1970).

Mainstream economics has problems of internal consistency or coherence and external consistency or correctness. It cannot explain the empirical evidence since it is based on axioms and it does not have a meso level of analysis – where the distributions of the agents' characteristics are not normal but characterised by fat tails, a clear indication that the whole is not the sum of individual behaviours but something different, something complex. We thus find ourselves with models that are very reminiscent of Lucas' (1980: p. 709) computational economics and, at times, are capable of producing time series that are partly compatible with the macro-evidence, but certainly incompatible with the lower levels (micro and meso). Let us remember that macro-results can be generated by many different micro-behaviours and are normally 'robustly insensitive' to the details of micro-processes. Therefore, replicating a few macroscopic properties is not sufficient proof of validation, and erroneous micro-foundations can lead to unrealistic policy implications; micro-foundations must be based on micro-models capable of replicating individual behaviour, not on the ability to replicate aggregate outcomes.

The new ideas developed by complexity economics indicate that markets and economies tend to operate in far from equilibrium conditions, and that different agents should be individually modelled as autonomous, active, and interactive entities, capable of making decisions and not just reacting to a stimulus. They usually have incomplete information and they make mistakes, but they also have the capacity to learn and adapt. Strategic behaviour among heterogeneous interacting agents with incomplete information generates a network, a set of relationships.

The method of conventional economics is rooted in nineteenth-century physics, in the dynamics of equilibrium and its stability (for a historical survey, see Ingrao and Israel, 1991; chp. XII). The study of the economy from the point of view of complexity (i.e., of adaptive evolutionary systems characterised by emergence) does not permit forecasting exercises in the usual sense because (a) it observes equilibrium in terms of a probability distribution, not of a balancing point or stationary trajectory, and, because of interaction, (b) it takes account of the points of discontinuity generated by innovation and structural change. For this reason, the only admissible forecasts are limited to the short term and in scenario terms (i.e., conditional on structural change and boundary conditions).

As we have seen, Hahn shows that the AD model, being an axiomatic system, has no normative value, without even mentioning the SMD 'theorem'. Solow and Hanh (1997) then argue that reducing economic analysis to mathematical reasoning alone, as the DSGE do, does not make economic sense. Instead, ABM (Gallegati et al., 2024) manages to analyse the system of interrelationships between agents at several hierarchical levels through the analysis of nodes and the study of the topology of networks.

When a theory is based on axiomatised first principles, the resulting model is predetermined as a theorem follows from its axioms. As such, the model turns out to be defined and immutable, as suitable for a natural law, thus apparently presenting itself as the most reliable formal tool for policy design. This consideration is valid as long as the model is consistent (consistency) and the world described by the model is a good approximation of the real one (correctness). But if the world changes, because the relationships between the fundamental quantities change, and the rigidity of the model does not take this possibility into account, then its reliability as a policy design tool is lost. The fact is that individuals may suffer the (normative) effects of theory when it affects policy makers but, after all, it is not because of this that individuals change their patterns of preference, decision, and action. It is their networks of relationships and interactions that induce change and, therefore, the world changes when phenomena emerge from below that we can neither predict nor explain solely by looking at the behaviour of heterogeneous individuals; much less can we do so by axiomatising a reductionist theory of action based on first principles. Models of axiomatic theories are reduced to formal exercises with which, at most, we can describe the world as we would like it to be rather than represent the world as it is.

This Element deals with a more general approach than the so-called *mainstream* approach: namely, the complexity approach, wherein the economy is an emergent system that develops and changes structurally over time. This is well represented by analyses on innovation, economic development, and structural change that treat the economy as a complex system (Solomon, 2007; Delli Gatti et al., 2010; Mikulecky, 2001; Holling, 2001; Israel, 2005; Farmer and Geanakoplos, 2008; Ladyman et al., 2012; Lavoie, 1989; Phelan, 2001; Pietronero, 2008).

Complexity economics can be read as an evolution of equilibrium economics to non-equilibrium. And since non-equilibrium contains equilibrium, complexity contains the Arrow–Debreu theory. It is therefore the beginning of a new research project, if not a new paradigm. There is therefore much work to be done, and we hope that readers will join the effort.

List of Acronyms

ABM	agent-based model/modelling
AD	Arrow–Debreu
BM	Boldrin–Montrucchio
CAS	complex adaptive system
DGP	data-generating process
DSGE	dynamic stochastic general equilibrium
HANK	Heterogenous Agents New Keynesian
NK-DSGE	New Keynesian DSGE
RA	Representative Agent
RBC	real business cycle
SFC	stock-flow consistent
SMD	Sonnenschein–Mantel–Debreu
SOC	self-organised criticality

References

Ackerman, F., (2002), Still Dead After all These Years: Interpreting the Failure of General Equilibrium Theory, *Journal of Economic Methodology*, 9(2): 119–139.

Akerlof, G. A., (2020), Sins of Omission and the Practice of Economics, *Journal of Economic Literature*, 58(2): 405–418.

Alexander, S. (1920), *Space, Time and Deity*, The Humanity Press.

Anderson, P. W., (1972), More is Different, *Science*, 177(4047): 393–396.

Angrist, J., and Pischke, J.-S., (2017), Undergraduate Econometrics Instruction: Through Our Classes, Darkly, *Journal of Economic Perspectives*, 31(2): 125–144.

Antonelli, C., (2011), *Handbook on the Economic Complexity of Technological Change*, Edward Elgar.

Antonelli, C., and Ferraris, G., (2017), The Creative Response and the Endogenous Dynamics of Pecuniary Knowledge Externalities: An Agent Based Simulation Model, Department of Economics and Statistics Cognetti de Martiis. Working Papers, N. 201717, University of Turin, Italy.

Aoki, M., and Yoshikawa, H., (2006), *Reconstructing Macroeconomics: A Perspective from Statistical Physics and Combinatorial Stochastic Processes*, Cambridge University Press.

Arrow, K., (1994), Methodological Individualism and Social Knowledge, *The American Economic Review*, 84(2): 1–9.

Arrow, K. J., and Debreu, G., (1954), Existence of an Equilibrium for a Competitive Economy, *Econometrica*, 22(3): 265–290.

Arrow, K. J. and Hahn, F. H., (1971), *General Competitive Analysis*, Holden-Day, Inc.

Arthur, W. B., (1989), Competing Technologies, Increasing Returns, and Lock-in by Historical Events, *Economic Journal*, 99(394): 116–131.

Arthur, W. B., (1999), *Complexity and the Economy*, Oxford University Press.

Arthur, W. B., (2013), *Increasing Returns and Path Dependence in the Economy*, Michigan.

Arthur, W. B., (2021), Foundations of Complexity Economics, *Nature Reviews Physics*, 3: 136–145.

Arthur, W. B., Durlauf, S. N., and Lane, D. A., (1997), *The Economy as an Evolving Complex System*, Addison-Wesley.

Ashby, W. R., (1947), Principles of the Self-Organizing Dynamic System, *Journal of General Psychology*, 37(2): 125–128.

Axtell, R., (2001), Zipf Distribution of US Firm Sizes, *Science*, 293(5536): 1818–1820.

Axtell, R., Kirman, A. P., Couzin, I. D., Fricke, D., Hens, T., Hochberg, M. E., Mayfiled, J. E., Schuster, P., and Sethi, T., (2016), Challenges of Integrating Complexity and Evolution into Economics, in Wilson, D. S., and Kirman, A. P., (eds), *Complexity and Evolution: Toward a New Synthesis for Economics*, Strüngmann Forum Reports, vol. 19, pp. 65–82.

Bak, P., Chen, K., Scheinkman, J. A., and Woodford, M., (1993), Aggregate Fluctuations from Independent Sectoral Shocks: Self-Organized Criticality in a Model of Production and Inventory Dynamics, *Ricerche Economiche*, 47(1): 3–30.

Bak, P., Paczuski, M., and Shubik, M., (1996), Price Variations in a Stock Market with Many Agents, *Physica A: Statistical Mechanics and its Applications*, 246 (3–4): 430–453.

Bak, P., Tang, C., and Wiesenfeld, K., (1987), Self-Organized Criticality: An Explanation of $1/f$ Noise. *Physical Review Letters*, 59(4): 381–384.

Bargigli, L., (2017), *Econometric Methods or Agent-Based Model*, in Gallegati, M., Palestrini, A., and Russo, A., et al., (eds.), *Introduction to Agent-Based Economics*, Academic Press.

Bargigli, L., di Iasio, G., Infante, L., Lillo, F., and Pierobon, F., (2013), The Multiplex Structure of Interbank Networks, *SSRN* (November 11). https://ssrn.com/abstract=2352787; http://dx.doi.org/10.2139/ssrn.2352787.

Barone, E., (1908), Il Ministro della Produzione nello Stato Collettivista, Giornale degli Economisti, Sept./Oct., 2, pp. 267–293, 392–414. Translated as 'The Ministry of Production in the Collectivist State', in von Hayek, F., ed. (1935), *Collectivist Economic Planning*, pp. 245–290; reprinted in R. Marchionatti, ed., (2004), *Early Mathematical Economics, 1871–1915: The Establishment of the Mathematical Method in Economics*, v. IV, Taylor & Francis, pp. 227–263.

Battiston, S., Delli Gatti, D., Gallegati, M., Greenwald, B. C. N., and Stiglitz, J. E., (2007), Credit Chains and Bankruptcy Propagation in Production Networks, *Journal of Economic Dynamics and Control*, 31(6): 2061–2084.

Bedau, M. A., (1997), Weak Emergence, *Philosophical Perspectives*, 11: 375–399.

Beinhocker, E., (2006), *The Origin of Wealth: Evolution, Complexity, and the Radical Remaking of Economics*, Penguin Random House.

Benes, J., Kumhof, M., and Laxton, D., (2014), *Financial Crises in DSGE Models: A Prototype Model*. IMF Working Paper, WP14/57.

Benhabib, J., and Day, R. H., (1981), Rational Choice and Erratic Behaviour, *The Review of Economic Studies*, 48(3): 459–471.

Bischi, G. I., (2012), Modelli Dinamici per le Scienze Sociali, in Fano, V., Giannetto, E., Giannini, G., and Graziani, P. (eds.), *Complessità e Riduzionismo*, INSOMNIA Epistemologica, pp. 7–21.

Bischi, G. I., Dawid, H., Dieci, R., and Matsumoto, A. (2017), Introduction to the special issue 'Nonlinear Economic Dynamics'. *Journal of Evolutionary Economics*, 27(5): 825–830.

Blaug, M., (2003), The Formalist Revolution of the 1950s, *Journal of History and Economic Thought*, 25(2): 145–156.

Bloch, H., and Metcalfe, S. (2011), Complexity in the Theory of the Developing Firm, in Antonelli, C., ed., *Handbook on the Economic Complexity of Technological Change*, Edward Elgar.

Blume, L., and Durlauf, S., (2000), *The Interactions-Based Approach to Socioeconomic Behavior*, Wisconsin Madison: Social Systems, Working papers Nr. 1.

Boldrin, M., and Montrucchio, L., (1986), On the Indeterminacy of Capital Accumulation Paths, *Journal of Economic Theory*, 40(2): 26–39.

Bookstaber, R., and Kirman, A. P., (2018), Modeling a Heterogeneous World, in Hommes, C., and LeBaron, J., (eds.), *Handbook of Computational Economics*, Vol. 4, pp. 769–795, Elsevier.

Brady, M. E., (2018), Given B. De Finetti's Conclusion that 'Probability (Objective) Does not Exist', Then Rational Expectations Does Not Exist Either, *SSRN*, https://papers.ssrn.com/sol3/papers.cfm?abstract_id=3282452.

Brinley, T., (1991), Alfred Marshall on Economic Biology, *Review of Political Economy*, 3(1): 1–14.

Brunk, G. G., (2001), Self-Organized Criticality: A New Theory of Political Behaviour and Some of Its Implications, *British Journal of Political Science*, 31(2): 427–445.

Buchanan, M., (2007), *The Social Atom: Why the Rich Get Richer; Cheaters Get Caught, and Your Neighbor Usually Looks Like You*, Bloomsbury.

Buiter, Willem H., (2009), The Unfortunate Uselessness of Most 'State of the Art' Academic Monetary Economics (March 6). *VoxEU, Research-based policy analysis and commentary from leading economists*. https://ssrn.com/abstract=2492949.

Caldarelli, G., Battiston, S., Garlaschelli, D., and Catanzaro, M., (2004), Emergence of Complexity in Financial Networks, in Ben-Naim, E., Frauenfelder, H., and Toroczkai, Z. (eds.), *Complex Networks. Lecture Notes in Physics*, vol 650. Springer, pp. 399–423.

Cariani, P., (1991), Emergence and Artificial Life, in Langton, C. G, Taylor, C., Farmer, J. D., and Rasmussen, S., (eds.), *Artificial Life II*, Addison-Wesley, pp. 775–796.

Cass, D., (1965), Optimum Growth in an Aggregative Model of Capital Accumulation, *Review of Economic Studies*, 32(3): 233–240.

Castañeda, G., (2021), *The Paradigm of Social Complexity. Vol. I: An Alternative Way of Understanding Societies and their Economies*, Centro de Estudios Espinosa Yglesias.

Castañeda, G., (2022), *The Paradigm of Social Complexity. Vol. II: Computational Models, Validation, and Applications*, Centro de Estudios Espinosa Yglesias.

Casti, J. L., (1997), *Would-Be Worlds: How Simulation is Changing the Frontiers of Science*, Wiley.

Cobb, C. W., and Douglas, P. H., (1928), A Theory of Production, *American Economic Review*, 18(1): 139–165.

Colasante, A., (2017), Experimental Economics for ABM Validation, in Gallegati, M, Palestrini, A., and Russo, A., et al., (eds.), *Introduction to Agent-Based Economics*, Academic Press, pp. 143–162.

Cont, R., (2001), Empirical Properties of Asset Returns Stylized Facts and Statistical Issues, *Quantitative Finance*, 1: 223–236.

Crick, F., (1994), *The Astonishing Hypothesis*, Simon and Schuster

Crow, J. F., (1955), *General Theory of Population Genetics: Synthesis*. Cold Spring Harbor Quantitative Symposium on Biology 20, 54–59.

Damper, R. I., (2000), Editorial for the Special Issue on 'Emergent Properties of Complex Systems': Emergence and Levels of Abstractions, *International Journal of Systems Science*, 31(7):811–818.

David, P. A., (2000), Path Dependence, its Critics and the Quest for 'Historical Economics', in Garrouste, P., and Ioannides., S., (eds.), *Evolution and Path Dependence in Economic Ideas: Past and Present*, Edward Elgar Publishing, chapter 2.

Delli Gatti D., Gaffeo, E., and Gallegati, M., (2010), Complex Agent-Based Macroeconomics: A Manifesto for a New Paradigm, *Journal of Economic Interaction and Coordination*, 5(2): 111–135.

De Finetti, B., (1931), Sul significato soggettivo della probabilità, *Fundamenta Mathematicae*, Warszawa, T. XVII: 298–329.

De Vroey, M., (2015), *A History of Macroeconomics from Keynes to Lucas and Beyond*, Cambridge University Press.

Debreu, G., (1959), *Theory of Value: An Axiomatic Analysis of Economic Equilibrium*, Cowles Foundation for Research in Economics at Yale.

Debreu, G., (1974), Excess Demand Functions, *Journal of Mathematical Economics*, 1(1): 15–21.

Delli Gatti, D., Gaffeo, E., Gallegati, M., Giulioni, G., Kirman, A., Palestrini, A., and Russo, A., (2007), Complex Dynamics and Empirical Evidence, *Information Sciences*, 177 (5): 1204–1221.

Delli Gatti, D., Gaffeo, E., Gallegati, M., Giulioni, G., and Palestrini, A., (2008), *Emergent Macroeconomics: An Agent-Based Approach to Business Fluctuations*, Springer.

Delli Gatti, D., Gallegati, M., Greenwald, B. N. C., Russo, A. and Stiglitz, J. E., (2009), Business Fluctuations and Bankruptcy Avalanches in an Evolving Network Economy, *Journal of Economic Interaction and Coordination*, 4: 195–212.

Delli Gatti, D., Gallegati, M., and Minsky, H. P., (1994), Financial Institutions, Economic Policy, and the Dynamic Behavior of the Economy, Working Paper n. 126, Levy Economics Institute of Barde College.

Di Guilmi, C., Landini, S., and Gallegati, M., (2017), *Interactive Macroeconomics: Stochastic Aggregate Dynamics with Heterogeneous and Interacting Agents*, Cambridge University Press.

Dosi, G., (1982), Technological Paradigms and Technological Trajectories: A Suggested Interpretation of the Determinants and Directions of Technical Change, *Research Policy*, 11(3): 147–162.

Dosi, G., (2023), *The Foundations of Complex Evolving Economies*, vol. I, Oxford University Press.

Duhem, P., (1954), *The Aim and Structure of Physical Theory*, Princeton University Press.

Edgeworth, F. Y., (1881), *Mathematical Psychics: An Essay on the Application of Mathematics to the Moral Sciences*, C. Kegan Paul and Co.

Farmer, J. D., Geanakoplos, J., (2008), The Virtues and Vices of Equilibrium and the Future of Financial Economics, *Complexity*, 14(8): 11–38.

Felipe, J., and Fisher, F., (2003), Aggregate Production Function: What Applied Economists Should Know, *Metroeconomica*, 54(2–3): 208–262.

Feller, W., (1957), *An Introduction to Probability Theory and its Applications* (2nd ed.), John Wiley.

Feynmann, R. P., (2002), Il piacere di scoprire, Adelphi, Milano Giberti G. transl.– Carl Feynman and Michelle Feynman (1999) *The Pleasure of Finding Things Out*, Perseus Book, US.

Fischer, M. M., and Fröhlich, J., (eds.), (2001), *Knowledge, Complexity and Innovation Systems*, Springer-Verlag.

Fisher, F. M., (2013), *The Stability of General Equilibrium: What do we Know and Why is it Important?*, in Bridel, P., (ed.), *General Equilibrium Analysis: A Century After Walras*, Routledge.

Fitoussi, J. P., (2013), *Le Théorème du Lampadaire*, Les Liens qui Libèrent.

Foley, D. K., (1994), A Statistical Equilibrium Theory of Markets. *Journal of Economic Theory*, 62(2): 321–345.

Foley, D. K., (1996), Statistical Equilibrium in a Simple Labor Market, *Metroeconomica*, 47(2): 125–147.

Foley, D. K., (2003), 'Statistical Equilibrium in Economics: Method, Interpretation, and an Example', in *General Equilibrium: Problems and Prospects*, Hahn, F., and Petri, F., (eds.). Routledge Siena Studies in Political Economy. Taylor & Francis, chapter 4.

Forni, M., and Lippi, M., (1997), *Aggregation and the Microfoundations of Dynamic Macroeconomics*, Clarendon Press.

Foster, J., and Metcalfe, S., (2009), Evolution and Economic Complexity: An Overview, *Economics of Innovation and New Technology*, 18(7): 607–610.

Fraenken, K., (2006), *Innovation, Evolution and Complexity Theory*, Edward Elgar.

Friedman, M., (1969), *Optimum Quantity of Money*, Aldine Publishing Company.

Gabaix, X., (2009), Power Laws in Economics and Finance, *Annual Review of Economics*, 1: 255–294.

Gallavotti, G., (2016), Ergodicity: a Historical Perspective: Equilibrium and Nonequilibrium. *The European Physical Journal H*, 41(3): 181–259.

Gallegati, M., (1994), Composition Effect and Economic Fluctuations, *Economic Letters*, 44(1–2): 123–126.

Gallegati, M., Landini, S., and Gallegati, G. (2024), *Agent-Based Modelling: A Tool for Complexity*, Cambridge Elements in Complexity and Agent-based Economics, Cambridge University Press.

Gallegati, M., Palestrini, A., and Russo, A., (2017), *Introduction to Agent-Based Economics*, Academic Press.

Garegnani, P., (1970), Heterogeneous Capital, the Production Function and the Theory of Distribution, *The Review of Economic Studies*, 37(3): 407–436.

Gell-Mann, M., (1994), *The Quark and the Jaguar, Adventures in the Simple and the Complex*, Little, Brown and Company.

Georgescu-Roegen, N., (1970), The Entropy Law and the Economic Problem, Conference held on December 3rd 1970, Department of Economics, The Graduate School of Business and Office for International Programs, University of Alabama; Published in *The Ecologist*, 2, (7), 13–18, 1972.

Georgescu-Roegen, N., (1971), *The Entropy Law and the Economic Process*, Harvard University Press.

Gintis, H., (2006), The Dynamics of General Equilibrium, *The Economic Journal*, 117(523): 1280–1309.

Grandmont, J. M., (1985), On Endogenous Competitive Business Cycles, *Econometrica*, 53(5): 995–1045.

Greenwald, B. C., and Stiglitz, J. E., (1986), Externalities in Economies with Imperfect Information and Incomplete Markets, *The Quarterly Journal of Economics*, 101(2): 229–264.

Griliches, Z., (1979), Issues in Assessing the Contribution of Research and Development to Productivity Growth, *Bell Journal of Economics*, The RAND Corporation, vol. 10(1), pp. 92–116.

Grossman, S. J., and Stiglitz, J. E., (1980), On the Impossibility of Informationally Efficient Markets, *The American Economic Review*, 70(3): 393–408.

Hahn, F., (2002), The Dichotomy Once Again, *The European Journal of the History of Economic Thought*, 9(2): 260–267.

Hahn, F. H., (1965), 'On Some Problems of Proving the Existence of an Equilibrium in a Monetary Economy', in Hahn F. H., and Brechling, F. P. R., (eds.). *Theory of Interest Rates*. Macmillan, pp. 297–306.

Hahn, F. H., (1982), *Reflections on the Invisible Hand*, Warwick Economic Research Papers, n. 196.

Hall, R. E., (1976), *Notes on the Current State of Empirical Macroeconomics*, paper presented at the Workshop of Empirical Macroeconomics, Stanford.

Hamilton, W. D., (1964), The Genetical Evolution of Social Behavior, *Journal of Theoretical Biology* 7: 1–52.

Harcourt, R. F., (1972), *Some Cambridge Controversies in the Theory of Capital*, Cambridge University Press.

Hartley, J. E., (1997), *The Representative Agent in Macroeconomics*, Routledge.

Hildenbrand, W., (1994), *Market Demand: Theory and Empirical Evidence*, Princeton University Press.

Hodgson, G. M., (1993), The Mecca of Alfred Marshall, *The Economic Journal*, 103(417): 406–415.

Hoffman, H., and Payton, D. W., (2018), Optimization by Self-Organized Criticality, *Scientific Reports*, 8, 2358.

Holland, J. H., (1990), Emergent Models, in Scott, A. (ed.), (1998), *Emergence: From Chaos to Order*, Addison-Wesley.

Holling, C. S. (2001), Understanding the Complexity of Economic, Ecological, and Social Systems, *Ecosystems*, 4(5): 390–405.

Hommes, C., (2013), *Behavioral Rationality and Heterogeneous Expectations in Complex Economic Systems*, Cambridge University Press.

Ingrao, B. and Israel, G., (1991), *The Invisible Hand, Economic Equilibrium in the History of Science*, MIT Press.

Israel G. (2005), The Science of Complexity: Epistemological Problems and Perspectives, *Science in Context*, 18: 1–31.

Jakab, Z., and Kumhof, M., (2015), Banks are not Intermediaries of Loanable Funds – and Why this Matters, Bank of England, working paper 529.

Johnson, C. W., (2006), What are Emergent Properties and How Do They Affect the Engineering of Complex Systems? *Reliability Engineering & System Safety*, 91.

Kardar, M., (2007), *Statistical Physics of Particles*, Cambridge University Press.

Katz, J. S., (2016), What Is a Complex Innovation System?, *Plos One*,11(6); https://europepmc.org/article/med/27258040.

Keynes, J. M., (1921), *Treatise on Probability*, Macmillan & Co.

Keynes, J. M., (1936), *The General Theory of Employment, Interest and Money*, Macmillan.

Keynes, J. M., (1973), *The Collected Writings of J. M. Keynes*, vol. XIV, The General Theory and After. Part II. Defence and Development, Macmillan for the Royal Economic Society.

Kinchin, A. I., (1948), *Mathematical Foundations of Statistical Mechanics*, Dover Publications, Inc.

Kirman, A. P., (1989), The Intrinsic Limits of Modern Economic Theory: The Emperor has No Clothes, *The Economic Journal*, 99(395): 126–139.

Kirman, A. P., (1992), Whom or What Does the Representative Individual Represents?, *Journal of Economic Perspectives*, 6(2): 117–136.

Kirman, A. P., (2010) The Economic Crisis is a Crisis for Economic Theory, *CESifo Economic Studies*, 56(4): 498–535.

Kirman, A. P. (2019), *Complexity and Economics*, www.oecd.org/naec/new-economic-policymaking/NAEC_complexity_Alan_Kirman.pdf.

Knight, F. H., (1921), *Risk, Uncertainty and Profit*, Houghton Mifflin Company.

Koopmans, T. C., (1965), On the Concept of Optimal Economic Growth, in Johansen, J., (ed.), *The Econometric Approach to Development Planning*, North Holland.

Kubo, R., Toda, M., and Hashitsume, N., (1985), *Statistical Physics II: Nonequilibrium Statistical Mechanics*, Springer-Verlag.

Kydland, F. E., and Prescott, E. C., (1982), Time to Build and Aggregate Fluctuations, *Econometrica*, 50(6): 1345–1370.

Ladyman, J., Lambert, J., Wiesner, K., (2012), What is a Complex System? *European Journal for Philosophy of Science*, 3(1): 33–67.

Landau, L. D., and Lifshitz, E. M., (1980), *Statistical Physics*, Volume 5, Part I, Elsevier.

Landini, S., Gallegati, M., and Rosser, J. B. Jr, (2020), Consistency and Incompleteness in General Equilibrium Theory, *Journal of Evolutionary Economics*, 30(1): 205–230.

Laplace, P. S., (2007) [1902]. *A Philosophical Essay on Probabilities*. Translated by Truscott F. W. and Emory F. L., from the French 6th ed. (1840).

Lavoie, D., (1989), Economic Chaos or Spontaneous Order? Implications for Political Economy of the New View of Science, *Cato Journal*, 8: 613–635.

Lavoie, M., (2004), *L'Économie postkeynésienne*, La Découverte; English ed.: Introduction to Post-Keynesian Economics, Palgrave Macmillan (2006).

Lucas, R. E., Jr, (1972), Expectations and the Neutrality of Money, *Journal of Economic Theory*, 4(2): 103–124.

Lucas, R. E., Jr, (1976), Econometric Policy Evaluation: A Critique, *Carnegie-Rochester Conference Series on Public Policy*, Elsevier, 1(1): 19–46.

Lucas, R. E., Jr, (2003), Macroeconomic Priorities, *American Economic Review*, 93(1): 1–14.

Lucas, R. E., Jr, (1980), Methods and Problems in Business Cycle Theory, *Journal of Money, Credit, and Banking*, 14(4): 696–715.

Lucas, R. E., Jr, and Sargent, T. J., (1977), *Rational Expectations and Econometric Practice*, University of Minnesota Press.

Lunghini, G., (1991), Capitale, in Enciclopedia delle Scienze Sociali, Treccani. www.treccani.it/enciclopedia/capitale_%28Enciclopedia-delle-scienze-sociali%29/.

Majorana, E., and Mantegna, R. N. (2006), The value of statistical laws in physics and social sciences, in Bassani, G. F., (ed.), Ettore Majorana Scientific Papers. Springer.

Mantel, R. R., (1974), On the Characterization of Aggregate Excess Demand, *Journal of Economic Theory*, 7(3): 348–353.

Marshall, A., (1881), Review of F. Y. Edgeworth's Mathematical Psychics, *The Academy*, p. 457.

Marshall, A., (1890), *Principles of Economics*. 1 (1st ed.), Macmillan.

Mas-Colell, A., Whinston, M. D., and Green, J. R., (1995), *Microeconomic Theory*, Oxford University Press.

Massey, G. J., (2011), Quine and Duhem on Holistic Hypothesis Testing, *American Philosophical Quarterly*, 48(3): 239–266.

Mikulecky, D. C. (2001), The Emergence of Complexity: Science Coming of Age or Science Growing Old?, *Computers and Chemistry*, 25(4): 341–348.

Mill, J. S., (1843), *System of Logic* (8th Ed. 1872), Longmans, Green, Reader and Dyer.

Miller, J. H, and Page, S. E., (2007), *Complex Adaptive Systems: An Introduction to Computational Models of Social Life*, Princeton Studies in Complexity, Princeton University Press.

Mirowski, P., (1989), *More Heat Than Light*, Cambridge University Press.

Morgenstern, O., (1972), Thirteen Critical Points in Contemporary Economic Theory: An Interpretation, *Journal of Economic Literature*, 10(4): 315–335.

Morishima, M., (1984), *The Good and Bad Uses of Mathematics*, in Wiles, P. and G. North, (eds.), *Economics in Disarray*. Basil Blackwell, pp. 51–73.

Muth, J. F., (1961), Rational Expectations and the Theory of Price Movements, *Econometrica*, 29(3): 315–335.

Nash, J. F. Jr, (1950), Equilibrium Points in n-Person Games, *Proceedings of the National Academy of Science*, USA, 36, pp. 48–49.

Nicolis, G., and Nicolis, C., (2007), *Foundations of Complex Systems. Nonlinear Dynamics, Statistical Physics, Information and Prediction*, World Scientific.

Nicolis, G., and Prigogine, I., (1977), *Self-Organization in Non-Equilibrium Systems: From Dissipative Structures to Order through Fluctuations*, Wiley.

O'Connor, T., (1994), Emergent Properties, *American Philosophical Quarterly*, 31(2): 91–104.

O'Connor, T., (2021), Emergent Properties, Stanford Encyclopaedia of Philosophy; https://plato.stanford.edu/entries/properties-emergent/.

Pareto, V., (1896–1897), *Course d'Économie Politique*, Rouge.

Pareto, V., (1906), *Manuale di Economia Politica*, Società Editrice Libraria, Milano.

Parisi, G., (1999), Complex Systems: A Physicist's Viewpoint, *Physica A*, 263: 557–564.

Parisi, G., (2021), *In un Volo di Storni: Le meraviglie dei sistemi complessi*, Rizzoli.

Peters, O., (2019), The Ergodicity Problem in Economics, *Nature Physics*, Vol. 15, pp. 1216–1221.

Phelan, S. (2001), What is Complexity Science, Really?, *Emergence*, 3: 120–136.

Pietronero, L., (1998), *Il Semplice ed il Complesso dalla Fisica alla Biologia*, Frontiere della Vita Treccani. www.treccani.it/enciclopedia/il-semplice-e-il-complesso-dalla-fisica-alla-biologia_%28Frontiere-della-Vita%29/.

Pietronero, L., (2008), Complexity Ideas From Condensed Matter and Statistical Physics, *Europhysics News*, 39(6): 26–29.

Piñero, G. E., (2014), *Gödel. I Teoremi dell'Incompletezza*, RBA Italia Srl.

Poinsot, L., (1803), *Elements de Statique*, Kessinger Publishing.

Price, G. R., (1970), Selection and Covariance, *Nature*, 227, 520–521.

Prigogine, I., and Stengers, I., (1977), The New Alliance, *Scientia*, 71(12): 287.

Quine, W. V. O., (1951), Two Dogmas of Empiricism, *The Philosophical Review*, 60(1): 20–43.

Raatikainen, P., (2020), *Gödel Incompleteness Theorems*. https://plato.stanford.edu/archives/spr2021/entries/goedel-incompleteness/.

Ramsey, F. P., (1928), A Mathematical Theory of Saving, *The Economic Journal*, 38(152): 543–559.

Rizvi, S. A. T., (2006), The Sonnenschein–Mantel–Debreu Results after Thirty Years, *History of Political Economy*, 38: 228–245.

Romer, P. M., (1994), The Origins of Endogenous Growth, *Journal of Economic Perspectives*, 8(1): 3–22.

Roncaglia, A., (2005), *The Wealth of Ideas: A History of Economic Thought*, Cambridge University Press.

Rosen, R., (2012), *Anticipatory Systems, Philosophical, Mathematical, and Methodological Foundations*, Springer-Verlag.

Rosser, J. B. Jr, (2021), *Foundations and Applications of Complexity Economics*, Springer Nature.

Saari, D. G., (1992), The Aggregated Excess Demand Function and other Aggregation Procedures, *Economic Theory*, 2(3): 359–388.

Scheinkman, J. A., and Woodford, M., (1994), Self-Organized Criticality and Economic Fluctuations, *The American Economic Review*, Papers and Proceedings of the Hundred and Sixth Annual Meeting of the American Economic Association, 84(2): 417–421.

Schumpeter, J. A., (1947), *Capitalism, Socialism and Democracy*, Routledge.

Schumpeter, J. A., (1954), *History of Economic Analysis*, Routledge.

Schurer, A. P., Hegerl, G. C., Luterbacher, J., Brönnimann, S., Cowan, T., Tett, S. F. B, Zanchettin, D., and Timmreck, C., (2019), Disentangling the Causes of the 1816 European Year Without a Summer, *Environmental Research Letters*, 14(9).

Shaikh, A., (2016), *Capitalism: Competition, Conflict, Crisis*. Oxford University Press.

Simon, H., (1997), *Administrative Behavior: A Study of Decision-Making Processes in Administrative Organizations*, The Free Press.

Solomon, S., (2007), *Complexity Roadmap*, Institute for Scientific Interchange.

Smets, F., and Wouters, R., (2003), An Estimated Dynamic Stochastic General Equilibrium Model of the Euro Area, *Journal of the European Economic Association*, 1(5): 1123–1175

Solow, R. M., (1956), A Contribution to the Theory of Economic Growth, *The Quarterly Journal of Economics*, 70(1): 65–94.

Solow, R., and Hanh, F., (1997), *A Critical Essay on Modern Macroeconomic Theory*, MIT Press.

Sonnenschein, H., (1972), Market Excess Demand Functions, *Econometrica*, 40(3): 549–563.

Soros, G., (2013), Fallibility, Reflexivity, and the Human Uncertainty Principle, *Journal of Economic Methodology*, 20(4): 309–329.

Sraffa, P., (1932a), Dr. Hayek on Money and Capital, *The Economic Journal*, 2(165): 42–53.

Sraffa, P., (1932b), Money and Capital: A Rejoinder, *The Economic Journal*, 42(166): 249–251.

Sraffa, P., (1960), *Production of Commodities by Means of Commodities: Prelude to a Critique of Economic Theory*, Cambridge University Press.

Steels, L., (1991), *Towards a Theory of Emergent Functionality*, in Meyer, J. A., and Wilson, S. W., (eds.), From Animals to Animants, Proceedings of the First International Conference on Simulation and Adaptive Behavior, Bradford Books/MIT Press.

Stephan, A., (1998), Varieties of Emergence in Artificial and Natural Systems, *Zeitschrift für Naturforschung C*, 53(7–8): 639–656

Stiglitz. J. E., (2018), Where Modern Macroeconomics Went Wrong, *Oxford Review of Economic Policy*, 34(1–2): 70–106.

Stokey, N. L., and Lucas, R. E. Jr, (1989), *Recursive Methods in Economic Dynamics*, Harvard University Press.

Thurner, S., Hanel, R., and Klimek, P., (2018), *Introduction to the Theory of Complex Systems*, Oxford University Press.

Trichet, J.-C., (2010), *Reflections on the Nature of Monetary Policy Non-Standard Measures and Finance Theory*, Speech by Jean-Claude Trichet, President of the ECB, opening address at the ECB Central Banking Conference Frankfurt, 18 November 2010; www.ecb.europa.eu/press/key/date/2010/html/sp101118.en.html.

Von Neumann, J., and Morgenstern, O., (1947), *Theory of Games and Economic Behavior*, Princeton University Press.

Waldrop, M. M., (1993), *Complexity: The Emerging Science at the Edge of Order and Chaos*, Simon and Schuster.

Walras, L., (1874), *Éléments d'Économie Politique Pure, ou Théorie de la Richesse Sociale* (Elements of Pure Economics, or the Theory of Social Wealth, transl. W. Jaffé), (1899, 4th ed.; 1926, rev ed., 1954, Engl. transl.)

White, D., (2023), Adaptive Functions in an Agent-Based Model of an Economic System. *Adaptive Behavior*, 31(1): 21–34.

Wilson, G. W., and Pate, J. L., (1968), Ricardo's 93 Per Cent Labor Theory of Value: A Final Comment, *Journal of Political Economy*, 76(1): 128–136.

Woodford, M., (2003), *Interest and Prices*, Princeton University Press.

Acknowledgements

This Element analyses and studies in a simple way the possible transition from equilibrium economics to complexity economics, where time and history matter and the most unpredictable events happen emerging, as they often do in life, so S. L. dedicates this book to Claudia Gamba.

To Claudia,
even after 30 years,
wherever you have been,
wherever you stand and will be.

For all the comments and constructive criticism, we are indebted to Silvano Cincotti, Domenico Delli Gatti, Tiziana Di Matteo, Giovanni Dosi, Magda Fontana, Alan Kirman, Fabrizio Lillo, Valerio Lucarini, Rosario Mantegna, Salvatore Micciché, Luciano Pietronero, Flaminio Squazzoni, Francesco Sylos Labini, and, in particular, to Robert Axtell, Pietro Terna, and Leigh Tesfatsion.

Cambridge Elements

Complexity and Agent-Based Economics

Maria Enrica Virgillito

Sant'Anna School of Advanced Studies

Maria Enrica Virgillito is Associate Professor in Economics at the Institute of Economics, Sant'Anna School of Advanced Studies, Pisa, Italy where she coordinates the Seasonal School in "Agent-Based models in Economics". Her publications have been hosted in a number of international scientific peer-reviewed journals in the realms of complexity economics, institutional labour economics, evolutionary economics. She is Global Labour Organization Fellow and serves as Editor for the Macro and Development yearly issue of *Industrial and Corporate Change*, as Associate Editor for *Structural Change and Economic Dynamics* and for the *Review of Evolutionary Political Economy.*

About the Series

Elements in Complexity and Agent-Based Economics will present the state-of-the-art in complexity and agent-based economics with the aim of offering a systematic and easy-to-access thematic organization of both consolidated results, and the latest developments in the fields. Contributions are meant both as a support to scholarly research and as teaching tools.

Cambridge Elements

Complexity and Agent-Based Economics

Elements in the Series

Active Particles Methods in Economics: New Perspectives in the Interaction between Mathematics and Economics
Nicola Bellomo, Diletta Burini, Valeria Secchini and Pietro Terna

Complexity in Economics
Simone Landini, Giacomo Gallegati and Mauro Gallegati

A full series listing is available at: www.cambridge.org/ECAE

For EU product safety concerns, contact us at Calle de José Abascal, 56–1°, 28003 Madrid, Spain or eugpsr@cambridge.org.

www.ingramcontent.com/pod-product-compliance
Ingram Content Group UK Ltd.
Pitfield, Milton Keynes, MK11 3LW, UK
UKHW022146080726
473066UK00010B/795

* 9 7 8 1 0 0 9 5 4 7 7 3 4 *